Playtime Poets
Edited by Allison Jones

First published in Great Britain in 2008 by:
Young Writers
Remus House
Coltsfoot Drive
Peterborough
PE2 9JX
Telephone: 01733 890066
Website: www.youngwriters.co.uk

All Rights Reserved

© Copyright Contributors 2008

SB ISBN 978-1 84431 509 3

Foreword

Young Writers was established in 1991 and has been passionately devoted to the promotion of reading and writing in children and young adults ever since. The quest continues today. Young Writers remains as committed to the nurturing of poetic and literary talent as ever.

This year's Young Writers competition has proven as vibrant and dynamic as ever and we are delighted to present a showcase of the best poetry from across the UK and in some cases overseas. Each poem has been selected from a wealth of *Little Laureates* entries before ultimately being published in this, our sixteenth primary school poetry series.

Once again, we have been supremely impressed by the overall quality of the entries we have received. The imagination, energy and creativity which has gone into each young writer's entry made choosing the poems a challenging and often difficult but ultimately hugely rewarding task - the general high standard of the work submitted ensured this opportunity to bring their poetry to a larger appreciative audience.

We sincerely hope you are pleased with this final collection and that you will enjoy *Little Laureates Playtime Poets* for many years to come.

Contents

Amy Evans	1
Alexandra O'Malley (9)	1
Elsie Seun Aluko (8)	2
Grace Whittaker (10)	3

Arundel CE Primary School, Arundel

Katarina Peters (9) & Phoebe Phillips (10)	4
Liam Wells & Tom Olliver-Boddington (9)	4
Marcus Lee (9)	5
Emily Prideaux & Katy Knight (9)	5
Joseph Ward & Joss Hole (9)	6
Alex Reeves (8)	6
Lorna Cox & Esmé Durlston-Powell (9)	7
Leon Harris & William Telford (9)	7
Natalie Kerry (9)	8
Hannah McNeill, Ellis Wilkinson-Harvey, Harrison Doughty & Mariah Keen (9)	8
Ieuen Rees (8)	9
Charlie Weller (9)	9
Storm Tester, Charlie Bizzell, Ben Roberts (9) & Saskia Marsh (10)	10
Stella Swain (9)	11
Lilium Wikinson-O'Dwyer, Lucy Massie, Emily Merriott (8) & Skye Mansbridge (9)	12
Will Lloyd (8)	12
Sam Munro & Nathan Black (9)	13

Ashover Primary School, Ashover

Freya Clarke (9)	13
Poppy Hanauer (10)	14

Cloverlea Primary School, Altrincham

Joshua Worrall (7)	15
Seren Murphy (7)	16
Lucy Taylor (7)	16
Shannan O'Donnell (7)	17
Leon Cann (7)	17

Olivia Kelly-Bradshaw (7)	18
Sam Blackburn (7)	18
Michael Norris (7)	19
Maleace Hughes (7)	19
Hannah Roberts (7)	20
Michael Teague (8)	21
Matthew Reynolds (8)	22
Emilly Hall (7)	23
Maya Hattori (7)	24
Jasmin Notley (7)	25
Bethan Radford (7)	26
Charlie Yates (7)	27
Max Landsborough (8)	28
Billy Atack (7)	29
Daniel Cocker (7)	30
Megan Thomson (8)	31
Sam Sellwood-Richards (7)	32

Cromer Junior School, Cromer

Kirsty Clarke (11)	32
Bethany Johns (10)	33
Laura Smith (10)	34
Chloe Lee (10)	35
Hannah Carter (11)	36
Alice Wreford (10)	37
Robert Cox (11)	38
Gemma Harris (10)	39
Karly Dynes (10)	40
Jordanna Yeo (10)	41

Cwmafan Junior School, Port Talbot

Thomas Holroyd (11), Christopher Howe & Ieuan Simpkins	42
Aaron Diplock & Ross Smith (11)	42
Tomas O'Leary, Jack Phillips (10) & Kieran Hooper	43
Caitlyn Thomas & Olivia Rees (10) & Megan John (11)	43
Michaela Wood (10), Katie Murphy & Emily Jones	44
Bethan Moore & Zoe Tanner	44
Rhydian Bowden & Carwyn Davies	44
Darcie Talbot & Sophie Slade (11)	45
Denni-Tyla Bell (10), Molly Pickering & Chelsea Griffin	45

Jake Phillips & Emily Fisher (11)	45
Olivia Martin & Gethyn Hopson (10)	46
Holly McNeil	46
Thomas Ebley	46
Thomas Holroyd, Christopher Howe & Ieuan Simpkins	47
Demi Davies	47

Dunchurch Junior School, Dunchurch

Elliott Morgan (9)	47
Jake Menesse (11)	48
Erin Bashford (10)	49
Amy Thomas (10)	50
Dan Hyslop (9)	50
Sarah Jenkins (10)	51
Adam Cheney (10)	51
Kayleigh May Manning (10)	52
Florence Harris (10)	52
Philip Dickinson (9)	53
Corey Bevan (9)	53
Imogen Fancourt (10)	54
Sam Burn (10)	54
Sayla Maule (10)	55
Shanil Rathod (10)	55
Carys Ireson (9)	56
Alexander Holton (9)	56
Luke Norman (10)	57
Harriet Smith (9)	57
Ariane Turner (9)	58
Declan Turnbull (10)	58
Oliver Smith (10)	59
Calum O'Keefe (10)	59
Josh Ireson (11)	60
Lawrence Baker (10)	60
Shane Jenkinson (11)	61
Matthew Rush (10)	61
Jamie Ross (10)	62
Ross Carlton (9)	62
Alex Smith (10)	63
Ben Malin (9)	63
Hannah Downes (10)	64
Matthew Dunkley (9)	64

Michelle Murdoch (10)	65
Ashley Fiedler (9)	65
Lauren Peel (10)	66
Marcus Coles (9)	66
Thomas Oglethorpe (10)	67
Luke Menesse (9)	67
Rhys Warren (10)	68
Katie Mackenzie (10)	68
Courtney Phillips (10)	69
Ruby Hartland (9)	69
Joe Fletcher (11)	70
Joshua Whitington (9)	70
Lauren Love (10)	71
Imogen Slinn (10)	71
Tom Crathorne (11)	72
Eve Palmer (10)	72
Emily March (10)	73
Richard Massie (9)	73
Samantha Townsend (10)	74
Samuel Barnes (9)	74
Jo-Jo Pendlebury (10)	75
Sara Pawsey (9)	75
Jake Lewis (10)	76
Alex James Smith (10)	76
Harry Dibsdale (10)	77
Chelsea Lloyd (10)	77
Isabel Sharratt (10)	78
Jessica Armitage (10)	78
Ben Williamson (11)	79
Eleanor Jones (10)	79
Shannon Moor (10)	80
Jessica Thompson (10)	81
Ellie Smith (10)	82
Gemma Trodd (10)	83
Isabel Parsons (10)	84
Alice Hargreaves (10)	84
Woody Woodbridge (10)	85

Millfield Primary School, North Walsham

Courtney Cowens (8)	85
James Turner (8)	86

Hannah Richards (8)	86
James Maisner (8)	87
Luke Watling (8)	87

Our Lady & St Michael's RC Primary School, Abergavenny

Jemaica Bermas (8)	88
Jojo Arthur (8)	88
Oliver Tod (8)	88
Rosanna Williams (8)	89
Moira Taylor (8)	89
Jacob Pearl (9)	89
Ella Walsh (8)	90
Morgan Lewis (8)	90
Talitha Morrish (8)	90
Morgan Hopkins (8)	91
Anne Carrett (8)	91
Daniel Taylor (8)	91
Olivia Griffiths (8)	92
Maria James (8)	92
Catriona Baker (8)	92
Jack Meredith (8)	93
Alisha Skinner (9)	93
Matthew Gilbertson (8)	93
Maddie Davies (8)	94
Mariah Reyes (8)	94
Lucy Marsden (8)	94
Caszandra Erni (8)	95
Kieran Warburton (8)	95

St Margaret's CE Primary School, Crawley

Paige Newton	95
Oliver Murphy	96
Mia Bromige	96
Jack Donnelly (9)	97
Shelby Beeden	97
Lauren Thynne (9)	98
Andrew Hall (9)	98
Georgina Martin (10)	99
Shannon Bishop	99
Robyn Edwards	100
Lewis Jones (9)	100

Keanu Kellett (10)	101
Aimée Wheeler	101
Heidi Mousdell (9)	102
Kathryn Doggett (9)	103
Siannah Scopes (9)	104
Samantha Blakey (9)	104
Daisy Haggerty (10)	105
Aaliyah Kuyateh	105
Kate Turner	106
Zoe Young (10)	106
Georgina Reeves (9)	107
Georgia Harman (10)	107
Ella Pickford (9)	108
Ashleigh Hill (9)	109
Beth Murphy (9)	110
Sam Aston (9)	110
Sarah Soloman (10)	111
Zachary Lampey (9)	111
Samuel Lashwood	112
Christian Clark (9)	112
Matthew Clipperton (9)	112

St Mary's Primary School, Roughton

Alfie Woodrow (8)	113
Chloe Mason (8)	113
Phoebe Chambers (8)	113
Matthew Andrews (8)	114
Rhiannon Stanton (8)	114
Tequila Sayer (9)	115
Jordon Storey (9)	115
Bethany Griffin (8)	116
Chloe Lewis (8)	116

Saxlingham Nethergate Primary School, Norwich

Sophie Titlow (10)	117
Eliza Bolton (8)	117
Alana Emms (9)	118
Sammy O'Connor Balsillie (10)	118
Cameron Cawley (8)	119

Sele First School, Hexham
Eleanor Beadle (8)   119
Matthew Hutton (8)   120
Matthew Stokes (8)   121
Ben Shotton (8)   122
Oliver Slipman (8)   122
Kieran Stewart (9)   123
Oscar Goncalves (8)   123
Alice Merriman-Jones (8)   124
Heather Battye (8)   124
Kerri Tron (8)   125
Harrison Mann (8)   125
Stella Anastasiou (8)   126
Louis Edwards (8)   126
Hamish Forsyth (8)   127
James Carruthers (8)   127
Chloe Davey (8)   128
Megan Ashford (8)   128
Abigail Thomson (8)   129
Daniel Hope (8)   129
Luke James McCormick (9)   130
Dorothy Hakim (8)   130
Tony Crozier (8)   131
Hannah Pinkney (8)   131
Rachel Wood (8)   132
Luke Allman (8)   132
Erin Rodgers (8)   133
Jake McPherson (8)   133
Sam Ridealgh (8)   134
Calum Thomas (9)   134
Annie McCormick (8)   135
Holly Griffiths (8)   135
Catherine Brotherton (8)   136
Elizabeth Dracup (9)   136
James Hagon (8)   137
Roslyn Box (8)   137
Neema Mwande (9)   138
Alistair Scott (9)   138
Holly Atkinson (8)   139
Seamus Libretto (8)   139
Kirsty Brotherton (8)   140

Alexander Birkinshaw (8)	140
Erin Brook (8)	141
James Mitchell (8)	141
Cody Thompson (8)	142
Alex Kellas (8)	143
Thomas Jepson (8)	144
Olivia Fenwick (8)	144
Penny Parr (8)	145
Zoë Hardy (8)	145
Cameron Wilson (8)	146
Thomas Barnes (8)	146
Frannie Wise (8)	147
Ruby McCormick (8)	147
Hannah Harling (8)	148
Cameron Tibbles (8)	148
Grace Percival (8)	149
Amy Donaldson	149
Jake Dunlop (8)	149

Sporle CE Primary School, King's Lynn

Matthew Panes (8)	150
Sarah Hunt (8)	150
Cameron Willis (8)	150
Zoë Hembling (8)	151
Matthew Wilkins (9)	151
Harrison Bond (8)	151
Charlotte Simmons (9)	152
Samson Beech (9)	152

Turnditch CE Primary School, Turnditch

Joseph Seale (11)	152
Molly Jones (10)	153
Amy Poynton & Chloe Ryan (10)	153
Daisy Warzynska (11)	154
Louis Curtis & George Wagstaff (9)	154
Maria Webb (11)	155
Jack Sutton (10)	155
Emma White (10) & Lucy Phillips (11)	156
Daniel Breeze (10)	156

Wisborough Green Primary School, Wisborough Green

George Gibson	157
Bethany Tidd (11)	157
Alex Cooper	158
Jack Dixon (7)	158
Lucy Ansell	159
Emily Cornell (7)	159
Hollie James (10)	160
Grace Elsworth-Smith (7)	160
Lise Easton (11)	161
Lauren Porter (7)	161
Karis Montague (10)	162
Violet Nicholls (10)	163
Clive Allen (11)	164
Zsuzsi Overton	164
Max Dillon	165
Isobel Mayhew (7)	165
Callum Pearson (10)	166
Richard Mason (10)	166
Alice Warwick (10)	167
George Steere (10)	167
Joshua Rawlins (7)	168
Harry Baker (7)	168
Jacob Ball (7)	168
Laura Travers	169
James Cheal (8)	169
Natasha Calder Smith	169
Isobel Russel	170
Hannah Kirby (7)	170
Maddie Todd (9)	170
Harry Wheeler (9)	171
Lucy Travers (11)	171
Danielle Naughton (10)	172

The Poems

Untitled

Bells are ringing, bells are ringing,
Christ is born, Christ is born,
Join the celebrations, join the celebrations,
Christmas time! Christmas time!

We open presents, we open presents,
We are happy, we are happy,
We got what we had asked for,
We got what we had asked for,
Hip hip hooray! Hip hip hooray!

We say a huge thank you, we say a huge thank you,
For Christmas Day, for Christmas Day,
We're playing with our toys now,
We're playing with our toys now,
Christ is born! Christ is born!

Amy Evans

Parallels

Will children be hurt or sold,
Or will they have a family to love and hold?
Will they have to look in dustbins in the cold, wet street,
Or in a warm house for something to eat,
Like veg, meat or rotten fish
That's been lying there for weeks?
Will they have a soft bed where they can sleep,
Or a hard rock for a pillow and nightmares for dreams?
So when you're lying all cosy in your bed,
Just spare a thought in your head
For the children on the street, with no bed
And nothing to eat.

Alexandra O'Malley (9)

The Spring And The Summer Sun

The warm spring wind blows
As the coldness of winter goes.

When the sun appeared from behind a cloud
My happiness and glee were once more found.

Sky as blue as the pure sea
Brought new delight and joy to me.

My face grew as bright as light
It felt like there would be no more wars, no more fights.

The summer sun dazzled bright
So there came to be more light.

We had a picnic outside
The food tasted like chocolate of the finest kind.

'Dum diddle dum,' buzzed the bees
As they worked busily in the trees.

The spring wind and the summer sun
Should not end they've just begun.

My friends and I sat on the grass
We forget that we worried about the work in class.

Elsie Seun Aluko (8)

I Hate Jane!

I hate Jane
And she hates me too,
She wouldn't share her sweets
And then scared me shouting, *'Boo!'*

She thinks I am a baby
'Cause I like Winnie the Pooh,
She says my lunch at school is yuck
Because she thinks it's *goo!*

I took back the friendship bracelet,
She took back that lovely belt,
Enemies forever
So angry we both felt.

Next day the sun was shining,
We made friends just like that,
We gave back our special gifts,
And stopped fighting like cats!

We'll fall out more
And that's fine,
But wherever you go,
Just keep it in mind,
It happens nearly all the time
And really . . . it's fine!

Grace Whittaker (10)

We Are Here For You

Joseph Saturday is done
And the darkness falls from the wings of night,
As a feather is drifting downwards.

I see the lights of Arundel,
Gleam through the rain and the mist,
And a feeling of sadness for Joseph comes over me,

That my soul cannot resist.
A feeling of sadness and longing for my friend
And resembles the rain
Come read to me some poem,

Mr Simpson some simple and heartful lay,
That shall soothe this restless feeling,
And banish the thoughts of day.

When the hours of day are numbered,
And the voices of the night wake,
Always remember, Joseph my friend,
Emerald class is here for you.

Katarina Peters (9) & Phoebe Phillips (10)
Arundel CE Primary School, Arundel

Poem Of Happiness

Happiness has no end but sadness an end.
If happiness ended we would not have a long life
Because it would not be a life,
So don't let sadness get the best of you.
Just try to remember the good times you had,
Remember your heart is not made of stone but of love.
So let the tears trickle down your cheeks,
But let your smile show how happy and special
Your dad was to you.
Memories are forever
And Joseph, you will always have them of your dad.

Liam Wells & Tom Olliver-Boddington (9)
Arundel CE Primary School, Arundel

Joseph's Dad

As soft winds sweep away the days,
Joseph looks back on life
Through a haze of an Arsenal fan.
Remembers playgrounds, parks
And friends in childlike gaze that never ends.
The laughter in a game of throw and catch,
Shall memory ever attach . . .
To innocence in youthful eyes,
Catching the ball, to Joseph's dad's surprise.

Joseph's recall your first bike, last wreck,
Who picked you up, said, 'What the heck?'
Convinced you to try again.
You tried again and you got on fine.

So Joseph as a new friend to you,
I will help you chase away the blues.

Marcus Lee (9)
Arundel CE Primary School, Arundel

If You Didn't Have A Friend

(Joseph lost his father while he was in our class)

A friend is like a flower,
A primrose to be exact,
Or maybe a door that is always open,
Is a door that never shuts.
A friend is like an owl, both wonderful and wise,
A friend is like a light bulb that never goes out,
A friend is like a clock that never stops ticking
Or a blossom that is always in bloom.
Joseph, you truly will always be my friend
And I will always try and bloom for you.
What would the world be if we didn't have a friend?

Emily Prideaux & Katy Knight (9)
Arundel CE Primary School, Arundel

What Shall I Put In My Cupboard?
(Inspired by 'Magic Box' by Kit Wright)

I shall put in my cupboard a singing fox,
A chattering cat
And a Smackdown vs Raw game,
That is what I will put in my cupboard.

I shall place in my cupboard a swimming fish,
A cheeky monkey
And a dancing dog,
That is what I will put in my cupboard.

I shall put in my cupboard a roaring T-rex,
A gliding raptor
And a cafeteria cow,
That is what I will put in my cupboard.

I shall place in my cupboard a terrific tree house,
Lots of animals
And cuddly teddy bears,
That is what I will put in my cupboard.

I shall put in my cupboard a Ferrari F1 car,
A PSP and a Nintendo Wii,
And José Mourinho's brand new sack!
That is what I will put in my cupboard.

Joseph Ward & Joss Hole (9)
Arundel CE Primary School, Arundel

How Are You?

I hope you get better soon
Wrap yourself up in warm blankets
Put those feet in front of the fire
Have a nice hot, sweet cup of tea
Make yourself relax
Because I am there for you.

Alex Reeves (8)
Arundel CE Primary School, Arundel

My Happy Friendship With Joseph

In my dreams,
Joe is king,
In my dreams,
He's everything.

In my dreams,
He's very rich,
Joe's the best
On the football pitch.

In my dreams,
Things go right,
Nothing's dark,
Everything's bright.

Oh, if life was
Like dreams,
If only life was
Like dreams.

Lorna Cox & Esmé Durlston-Powell (9)
Arundel CE Primary School, Arundel

Hope Is Always There

Hope people never get sad when sad things happen.
And hope people are never lonely,
But when you are unhappy, think of the good times.
Never get angry about bad things,
Always be happy and never be sad.

This is my grave by the holly tree,
Remember me and always be strong at all times,
Never forget other people really care.

Leon Harris & William Telford (9)
Arundel CE Primary School, Arundel

Joseph My Friend - It Is Now Gone!

Joseph my mate,
Saturday is over,
The time has passed,
It is now gone.

You should think of happy moments
When he was here,
You should be happy,
He wouldn't have wanted you to be sad,
It is now gone.

You should know,
That whenever you get unhappy,
You should go to your friends in Emerald class,
They are always there for you,
It is now gone.

You still have your mum and your sisters,
Think of how the girls are feeling,
Especially your mum.

Natalie Kerry (9)
Arundel CE Primary School, Arundel

Poems Of Friendship

Time flies when you go by,
Nothing stays the same.
On Saturday you lost your daddy,
We may not understand how you are feeling,
We bring a special poem with love,
But there's one thing that stays the same,
That will be our friendship.

Hannah McNeill, Ellis Wilkinson-Harvey, Harrison Doughty & Mariah Keen (9)
Arundel CE Primary School, Arundel

Sunset

If you are down with a frown,
Turn the frown upside down and smile all around
And lift the sun up, so it can shine all around,
So the trees are greener
And the sky's blue.

The wind is calm
So come outside to play
And spread the joy all around.
Jump up and down and turn around
Climb all trees, smallest to tallest.
Shout out loud and listen to the birds
Singing a beautiful song.
The horses are eating, the cows mooing,
The sheep are sleeping and playing
The farm is a beautiful place.

Ieuen Rees (8)
Arundel CE Primary School, Arundel

Sorrow For Joseph, A Boy In My Class

Sadness, sadness everywhere,
We are sorry for the loss of your dad,
Because when he died,
All our hearts were broken.
So sadness, sadness everywhere,
So your mind and heart may be sad,
But you must remember those happy days,
Days with Dad cannot ever be forgotten,
Like going to the cinema and seeing James Bond.

Charlie Weller (9)
Arundel CE Primary School, Arundel

Thanks Joe!

Thanks Joe, for being a very good friend to us!
Life is like a game and someday that game must end.
We know what you have been through,
But this is about the time when you and Ben had a sleepover,
You went to see Casino Royale at the cinema.
We are always thinking of you, all the time.
We will always be there if you need someone to talk to,
If you need a hug.
Soon it will be our turn, but hopefully we won't know when.
We all remember the times when you rode your bike,
When you played football with your mates,
When you had a bad day, but remember we are always there for you.
When you're feeling down, we will never leave you.
Whatever the future may hold, we are here,
Sticking up for you and keeping you safe.
Your dad is always thinking of you and don't you forget it,
Thinking how proud he is of you,
For doing your best and being brave all the time.
Just think, one day you will see your dad again.
Keep happy because you still have your mum, Hannah
                                          and Charlotte,
They all love you and so does your dad.
But we are all here still with you, so don't blame it on yourself,
It's not your fault, so stay being happy.

**Storm Tester, Charlie Bizzell, Ben Roberts (9)
& Saskia Marsh (10)**
Arundel CE Primary School, Arundel

The Tunnel

Walking through a tunnel,
Through darkness blacker than night,
Surely it must have an end,
That's brighter than the brightest light.

Walking through a tunnel,
With wet, dripping walls,
Maybe I'm under
Some mysterious, wandering waterfalls.

Walking through a tunnel,
Colder than the North Pole,
It really is chilly,
Down in this dark, devilish hole.

Walking through a tunnel,
Dark, cold and wet,
How much deeper and darker underground
Does this tunnel get?

Walking through a tunnel,
Nearly at the end,
Always having hope,
Light and happiness,
Is round the next bend.

Stella Swain (9)
Arundel CE Primary School, Arundel

Life

Getting on with life is good,
It may be hard sometimes,
But you will get through it,
We, being,
Skye, Lil, Emily and Lucy
Will help you.

Getting on with life is good,
You will always get through life,
It's like a game of snakes and ladders,
You will go up sometimes
And sometimes you have to go down.
But eventually,
If you do not give up,
You will be a winner.

**Lilium Wikinson-O'Dwyer, Lucy Massie, Emily Merriott (8)
& Skye Mansbridge (9)**
Arundel CE Primary School, Arundel

Joseph's Dad

As soft wind sweeps away the days,
Joseph looks back on life through the haze.
Remember playgrounds, parks and friends,
In a childlike gaze that never ends.
The laughter in a game of catch,
Shall memory ever attach,
To innocence in youthful eyes,
Catching the ball to Dad's surprise.
Joseph will never forget,
As long as he remembers,
That joy of fun with his dad.

Will Lloyd (8)
Arundel CE Primary School, Arundel

His Sparkling Smile

In that smile
The world grows and glows
In that smile
A new world blossoms
In that smile
Earth - suffering hears the message
Of fire - pure transformation
Complete transformation.

Sam Munro & Nathan Black (9)
Arundel CE Primary School, Arundel

Sammy

Sammy the Crimp has a lovely huge cave,
But his brother is the King Sham's knave;
He kicks and scratches about the palace
Whilst Sammy, he wallows in malice.

Sammy keeps his room neat,
But his brother won't change a sheet.
Mum Crimp wasn't pleased,
So brother Joe, he ceased
And stormed out of the cave in a strop!

Sammy thought it wasn't nice,
Later his mum made a big pot of rice.
That cheered him up immensely,
But Joe just acted more fiercely!

Freya Clarke (9)
Ashover Primary School, Ashover

The Grimp

The Grimp lives in a deep, dark cave
His mum shouting at him to behave
'Wash your face, don't pick your nose,'
This is how it usually goes
All day and night it never stops
'Tidy your bedroom and put back those socks!'

The Grimp never listens to his mother
That's why they always fight with each other
'I've had enough of this horrible behaviour
I'm sending you to Bad Boys' Saviour!'
Bad Boys' Saviour was a terrible school
With ugly monster teachers that dribbled and drooled
With toilets that were too gruesome to describe
And classrooms full of little boy tribes
But out of the school came well behaved boys
With no fustle or bustle or awful noise
'Oh, I will be good as gold, I promise,' he said
'Too late, I'm looking forward to my rest in bed.'

Five months later out of the blue
Came a well behaved Grimp, wahoo!
The Grimp's mother jumped up and cried
'I now have a son that I can have with great pride!'

It just goes to show, it's no use being bad
You don't want to go to a school that's so mad!

Poppy Hanauer (10)
Ashover Primary School, Ashover

The Magic Box
(Based on 'Magic Box' by Kit Wright)

I will put in my box . . .

The blackest sun,
The reddest railway track,
The biggest, bluest bay.

I will put in my box . . .

The *bam* of a football hitting a crossbar,
The taste of juicy mango,
The *bang* of yellow lightning.

I will put in my box . . .

The roughness of a scaly lizard,
The smell of the runniest chocolate,
The sound of a lion roaring.

I will put in my box . . .

The biggest, reddest ant,
The greenest log,
The smallest giraffe.

My box is made out of water
And it has Europe in the corners.
It has coconut on the bottom.
The hinges are made out of jawbones of clowns.
It has stars in the middle.

Joshua Worrall (7)
Cloverlea Primary School, Altrincham

Magic Box
(Based on 'Magic Box' by Kit Wright)

I will put in my box . . .

The howl of a wolf on a stormy night,
The taste of chocolate ice cream on a summer day,
The fragile fragrance of flowers.

My box is crafted from gold and glass shaped as stars.
On the lid there are sparkles
With the whole universe underneath.
The corners are as soft as a cute kitten.

I shall fly in my box,
A swan flying right next to me,
All over Australia I will go.

Seren Murphy (7)
Cloverlea Primary School, Altrincham

Magic Box
(Based on 'Magic Box' by Kit Wright)

I will put in my box . . .

The roar of the wild waves on a windy night,
The crashing of thunder in the middle of the night,
The howl of a wolf on a stormy night.

My box is made from wood, grass, trees and flowers,
With rubies, gold and glittering diamonds.
Its hinges are shiny and golden.

I shall fly in my box,
In the bluest sky,
The birds are tweeting
And I feel as happy as the sky.

Lucy Taylor (7)
Cloverlea Primary School, Altrincham

I Will Put In My Box
(Based on 'Magic Box' by Kit Wright)

I will put in my box . . .

A roar of a wild tiger on a cold, dark night,
The taste of a vanilla ice cream,
The smell of a rose on a summer day.

I will put in my box . . .

The taste of a curry on a frosty, cold, dark night,
The sight of a shining light,
The smell of a beautiful rose bush.

My box is crafted from
Silver glitter,
Gold from granite with glitter and rubies,
With fairy dust in the corners
And yellow, shining stars on the lid.

I shall skate in my box on the slippery, shiny ice,
Then fly in the bluest, coldest sky,
Then swim in the bluest sea on the sunniest day.

Shannan O'Donnell (7)
Cloverlea Primary School, Altrincham

The Magic Box
(Based on 'Magic Box' by Kit Wright)

I would ice skate in my box on ice.
I would fly in my magic box above the clouds
                    and above the oceans.
When there was the reddest sun,
I would fly in my box to Vietnam.
I would go home in my magic box.

My box is fashioned from wet ice and gold.
I will ice skate on the cold, wet ice.
In my magic box there is water.
I will surf on the water in my magic box.

Leon Cann (7)
Cloverlea Primary School, Altrincham

The Magic Box
(Based on 'Magic Box' by Kit Wright)

I will put in my box . . .

The howl of a wolf on a stormy night,
The roar of the wild waves on a windy night,
The whack of a football hitting a goal,
The taste of chocolate yummy in your mouth,
The lizard in the middle of the night.

My box is made from grass, wood and flowers,
It smells like a summer day,
With rubies, shiny paper and shiny ribbon.
Its hinges are the shape of a sweet wood.

I shall skate in my box
On the shiniest ice and the slipperiest icy water
Over the white blanket and the sparkly star
With blue skates.

Olivia Kelly-Bradshaw (7)
Cloverlea Primary School, Altrincham

Magic Box
(Based on 'Magic Box' by Kit Wright)

I will put in my box . . .

The roar of the wild waves on a windy night,
The taste of horrible salty water in my mouth,
The bang of the fireworks.

My box is made from gold, glass and silver diamonds,
The smoke of the dragon
And the penguin waddling about.

I will ride my big blue and white bike in my box,
The big green trees swaying in the wind all around me,
The smoke from the smoky dinosaurs.

Sam Blackburn (7)
Cloverlea Primary School, Altrincham

The Magic Box
(Based on 'Magic Box' by Kit Wright)

I will put in my box . . .

The howl of a wolf on a stormy night,
The whack of a football hitting a goal,
The roar of the wild waves and waves on a windy night.

My box is made from diamonds on the sides
And gold on the lid,
With metal and even rubies,
The hinges are cold, slippy ice.

I shall run in my box,
The boiling hot sun shining on my head,
The birds are singing,
They are singing beautifully.

Michael Norris (7)
Cloverlea Primary School, Altrincham

The Magic Box
(Based on 'Magic Box' by Kit Wright)

I will put in my box . . .

A gleaming palace,
The jumpiest kangaroo
And a wish and a star.

My box is made of gleaming cobwebs,
Sparkling spiders and dragon's smoke,
With rubies on the lid.

I will stand like a statue in my box,
Then I will build a house, a gleaming house.
I will dance and have a party.

Maleace Hughes (7)
Cloverlea Primary School, Altrincham

The Magic Box
(Based on 'Magic Box' by Kit Wright)

I will put in my box . . .

The roar of a lion the colour of the sun,
The smell of air freshener on a winter night,
The taste of chocolate trickling down my throat.

I will put in my box . . .

The purr of a baby kitten on a spring night,
The sparkle of a silver diamond on a summer night,
The laughter of children playing in the park.

I will put in my box . . .

The sight of puppies eating dinner,
The taste of bitter crisps on a Saturday night,
The sight of people rushing through the town.

I will put in my box . . .

The thirteenth month and a pink sun,
The shiniest rainbow on an Atlantic beach,
The shiniest day in the whole wide world.

My box is crafted from silver diamonds
And the reddest rubies,
With golden apples on the lid and secrets in the corners.
Its hinges are the jawbones of dinosaurs.

Hannah Roberts (7)
Cloverlea Primary School, Altrincham

The Magic Box
(Based on 'Magic Box' by Kit Wright)

I will put in my box . . .

The taste of a ripe, sweet apple falling from the top of a tree
Into my hands.
The annoying sound of a dreadful toucan
In the middle of a foggy night,
The sight of a colourful rainbow on a hot summer's day.

I will put in my box . . .

The howl of a wolf crying for help
In the middle of a stormy night.

I will put in my box . . .

An orange zebra,
And a black and white striped lion,
And the shiniest star on the Earth's ground.

My box is decorated with the shiniest transparent glass,
With golden stars and the reddest rubies on the shiniest lid
And secrets in the corners.
Its hinges are made from an ancient cat's bone.

I shall play football in my box,
Then sit down on the softest seat.

Michael Teague (8)
Cloverlea Primary School, Altrincham

The Magic Box
(Based on 'Magic Box' by Kit Wright)

I shall put in my box . . .

The roar of a terrible tiger on a sunny day,
The water from the bluest sea,
The sweetness of a chocolatey lime.

I shall put in my box . . .

The scent of a small bluebell,
The taste of the greenest leek,
The crackling of a red-hot fire.

I shall put in my box . . .

The greenest leaves ever known,
The hottest day in the world,
The greyest, wettest mountains.

I shall put in my box . . .

A surfing ghost
And a man in a grave,
A thirteenth month
And a yellow ground.

My box is made from frantic fungus and rock,
With skateboards on the lid and penguins in the corners.
Its hinges are the greenest of grass.

Matthew Reynolds (8)
Cloverlea Primary School, Altrincham

The Magic Box
(Based on 'Magic Box' by Kit Wright)

I will put in my box . . .

The tweeting of a bird on a summer's day,
The chatting of children on a winter's night,
The purr of a newborn kitten on a spring day.

I will put in my box . . .

The taste of hot chocolate on a winter's eve,
The smoky smell of smoke on an autumn bonfire,
The golden mane of a lion on a windy day.

I will put in my box . . .

The stripy red lion skin,
The golden mane of a yellow tiger,
A summer garden with a pink-red sky.

My box is fashioned with rubies and yellow spots,
With the shiniest silver lid and fairies in the corners.
Its hinges are fairies' silky wings.

I shall sing songs in my box,
In the highest tower of a castle,
Then fall into the prince's arms.

Emilly Hall (7)
Cloverlea Primary School, Altrincham

The Magic Box
(Based on 'Magic Box' by Kit Wright)

I will put in my box . . .

A purr of a baby kitten on a spring night,
A taste of an ice cream on a summer's day,
A smell of a beautiful flower on a spring morning.

I will put in my box . . .

A bow-wow of a baby puppy on a Christmas night,
A sip of a spicy soup on a winter's night,
A smell of a green forest on a summer day.

I will put in my box . . .

A cowboy in a wheelchair
And a grandfather on a black horse.

My box is created from fluffy flowers and diamonds in the corners,
With gorgeous gold on the lid and lovely lavender in the corners.
Its hinges are the bones of a dog.

I shall fly in my box,
In the high cobalt sky of the wild forest,
Then smell the green forest,
The colour of the trees.

Maya Hattori (7)
Cloverlea Primary School, Altrincham

The Magic Box
(Based on 'Magic Box' by Kit Wright)

I will put in my box . . .

The taste of smooth, melty chocolate
The smell of hot, baked cookies
The sight of Big Ben from miles away
The feel of bumpy sandpaper
The squeaky mouse giving me a headache

My box is made from sparkling stars and flashing, red diamonds
With roses in the corners and a silken web.
My box is full of secret wishes skiing down mountains
With shiny snow.
It's so pretty from far, far away,
It's the prettiest sight in all the world.
Its hinges are made of pterodactyl nails.

I shall do cartwheels on my box
On the greenest grass.
I will also do handstands
And forward roly-polys.

Jasmin Notley (7)
Cloverlea Primary School, Altrincham

The Magic Box
(Based on 'Magic Box' by Kit Wright)

I will put in my box . . .

The softest, furry, cuddly blankie,
The melty taste of chocolate in my mouth
The colourful, beautiful rainbow.

I will put in my box . . .

A fragile fragrance of a flower,
A big bouncy ball,
The stinky stench of a pair of socks.

I will put in my box . . .

The tweeting of a bird on a summery day,
A swish of the waves,
Children laughing and shouting at a party.

I will put in my box . . .

Father Christmas leaving Easter eggs
The Easter bunny leaving presents,
The teacher making us play.

My box is made from silver and gold,
Rubies and jewels
And sparkly diamonds with sparkles.

I shall do gymnastics in my box
On the biggest hill with the greenest grass.
It will have petals for its hinges,
Secrets for friends
And toe bones for the stands.

Bethan Radford (7)
Cloverlea Primary School, Altrincham

The Magic Box
(Based on 'Magic Box' by Kit Wright)

I will put in my box . . .

The goldest sand on a desert island,
The meanest beast that kills people,
The blackest night with the whitest moon.

I will put in my box . . .

The vroom of a car in the middle of the night,
The taste of a melon on a hot summer day,
The smell of a burning bonfire.

I will put in my box . . .

A blue sun and yellow rain,
Green water and blue grass.

My box is made from the goldest gold,
The lid is made from the reddest rubies,
The corners are made from the shiniest silver.
Its hinges are made from the clearest glass.

I shall snowboard in my box
On the coldest mountain with the whitest snow
And there will be some pancakes and chocolate milkshake
For a snack.

Charlie Yates (7)
Cloverlea Primary School, Altrincham

The Magic Box
(Based on 'Magic Box' by Kit Wright)

I will put in my box . . .

The splash of water,
The sight of stars,
The taste of Cadbury's chocolate oozing in my mouth.

I will put in my box . . .

The sound of a singing dolphin,
The taste of hot chocolate on a winter's day
And the taste of a Hawaiian pizza.

I will put in my box . . .

The fifth season of a blue sun,
A slug with a shell
And trees with purple leaves.

My box is made from chocolate and candy that never melts,
With éclairs on the lid
And edible roses in the corners.
Its hinges are made from Cadbury's Celebrations.

I shall draw pictures in my box of a country,
Then go to Old Trafford to watch Manchester United play football.

Max Landsborough (8)
Cloverlea Primary School, Altrincham

The Magic Box
(Based on 'Magic Box' by Kit Wright)

I will put in my box . . .

A squeak of a guinea pig in the afternoon,
The sea whistling in the middle of the night,
A football hitting a net.

I will put in my box . . .

Spicy, sweet curry, very hot,
Shiny, gloomy, silvery ice covered in snow,
The soft stroke of the dog.

My box is crafted from metal and granite and ice,
With bright red rubies on the lid
And magic tricks in the corners.

I shall play football on the greenest grass,
I will dive in the bluest sea in Egypt,
I shall surf in the Atlantic Ocean.

Billy Atack (7)
Cloverlea Primary School, Altrincham

The Magic Box
(Based on 'Magic Box' by Kit Wright)

I will put in my box . . .

An ancient Greek box
A hard helmet
And the yummiest cheese pie

I will put in my box . . .

The first baby's tooth
The first car's wheel
The first French word

I will put in my box . . .

The bluest ocean
An ancient Greek book

My box is fashioned from
Ice and steel with stars on the lid
And secrets in the corners
Its hinges are the toe joints of dinosaurs.

Daniel Cocker (7)
Cloverlea Primary School, Altrincham

The Magic Box
(Based on 'Magic Box' by Kit Wright)

I will put in my box . . .

The purr of a kitten at night
The bark of a puppy jumping for food
The gleaming shine of a diamond

I will put in my box . . .

The tweet of a baby blue tit
The shine of spiderwebs in the moonlight
The gleam of a star

My box is made of spiderwebs and feathers
With hummingbirds on the lid
And fire on the hinges

In my box I shall ride a dolphin
Then have a beach party all month
And then stay at home.

Megan Thomson (8)
Cloverlea Primary School, Altrincham

The Magic Box
(Based on 'Magic Box' by Kit Wright)

I will put in my box . . .

The cracking of ice,
The rolling of Smarties on the floor,
The taste of hot chocolate on a sunny day.

I will put in my box . . .

Chocolatey chocolate cake,
The smell of a flower,
The swish of chocolate sauce.

I will rollerskate in my box,
I will climb trees in my box.

My box is crafted from diamonds and glittering rubies,
With a rainbow on the lid.

Sam Sellwood-Richards (7)
Cloverlea Primary School, Altrincham

No Home

I am on the street,
And I really reek,
I remember my home,
With my basket and bone,
My favourite part of my home,
Was when I licked at the throne,
I am in my box all alone,
Trying to forget about my home,
I know I was cheeky and times were rough,
But I miss when you called me your little ball of fluff,
But I want to go back, I want to go home,
I try to imagine a picture of my family at home . . .
But all I can see is me on my own.

Kirsty Clarke (11)
Cromer Junior School, Cromer

Homeless

I am homeless,
Nobody cares.
I am all tattered and smelly.
Nobody helps me.
I need a house.

You see me near the sea,
Picking crabs for me.
If only I had some money.
I am so sad and mad.

I have to suffer in the cold and rain,
I am in lots of pain.
All the people see me and say,
'Look at him, he's homeless,
He must be desperate for a house.
He has no money.'

People tease me with lots of food.
I am hungry and lonely.
I am disappointed.
I am homeless.

Bethany Johns (10)
Cromer Junior School, Cromer

Child Abuse

I hide under my bed,
I have tears in my eyes,
I look at my knees,
I see the bruises, the scratches,
I have had them all.

I get in my lumpy bed which is a blanket,
I blow out the candle and try to get comfy,
I finally get to sleep,
Then I get woken up by my mother storming up the stairs.

I stealthily scramble out of my blanket,
My knees wobble,
I fall down the stairs,
But no one cares.
I start to cook breakfast,
My tears fall in the pan of porridge.

My mouldy feet are cold on the kitchen tiles,
I stir the porridge,
Then I burn my finger on the gas.
It does not hurt very much,
As I have done it many times before.
I serve up the porridge.
Whilst I am doing that,
I think and say to myself,
Is there any hope for me?
I feel downhearted, dumped and neglected,
So I just get on with it.

Laura Smith (10)
Cromer Junior School, Cromer

Trapped

I was happy living where I was,
With nature all around me,
Then one day a trick, a trap,
End of all my joy and freedom.

Now my home is not a field, a forest or a jungle,
But caged in bars I live alone.
I roar, I growl, for them to let me out,
But no one ever hears me.
I'm forgotten, yet I am here.

This tiny bed is not enough,
And the small amount of food.
OK, there are some leaves around,
But not like back at home.

No space I have to jump around,
Just a tiny place to pace.
But I wonder if there's a point,
I hope they'll let me out!

I dream of being back at home,
With family and my friends,
But will they let me out?
Why should they rule me?

So I stay here,
Hoping, helpless,
But will they ever let me out?
Will I ever be free?

Chloe Lee (10)
Cromer Junior School, Cromer

I'm, If, I

I'm me
I'm I
I'm lonely
I'm a child

If only I was you
If only I was strong
If only I was clean
If only I was not where I am

I wish I had clothes
I wish I had a bed
I wish I had food
I wish I had a home

I hate it here
I hate life
I hate losing
I hate being me

I'm a child
If only I was not where I am
I wish I had a home
I hate being me . . .

I live in a place called Poverty.

Hannah Carter (11)
Cromer Junior School, Cromer

Working All Day

I have to work day and night,
I only have candles for light,
I have a burnt hand on my right,
I don't get sleep at night

It's boiling in the summer,
It's freezing in the winter,
I won't get any rest later,
I'm in pain without food or water

I can't go to school,
I don't have time to make myself look cool,
I have to work, no time for football,
No money for the family, how will we survive?

I'm stealing now to survive,
I have an illness too bad to explain,
I'm going to die on the lane,
On my way to work.

Alice Wreford (10)
Cromer Junior School, Cromer

Scared!

Restlessly running,
Away from him,
I hide, scared by him,
He chases everywhere.

He calls me names,
I find hard to ignore,
Nasty names,
Horrible names.

I cry at home,
I tell my mum,
He's threatening,
He's hitting me.

He doesn't care,
His mates all laugh,
At me!
How would you like to be bullied?

Robert Cox (11)
Cromer Junior School, Cromer

Child Poverty

I'm on the street,
Nowhere to go,
No house, no garden,
Only a little spot to sit.

I'm angry and sad,
I wish there were no fights,
My parents fought so I left,
They fought every day, every night.

I have ripped clothes,
Grazed knees, smelly hair.
I sing for money and steal a phone,
So I can play all alone.

The food I eat is very little,
I starve sometimes.

That's the story about me.

Gemma Harris (10)
Cromer Junior School, Cromer

One Knock, Two Knocks, Downfall

One knock, she broke her neck,
Two knocks, no big deal,
Downfall, can't move a muscle,
On the floor in agony.

Second pain,
Blood dripping from her neck,
Tears dropping down her face,
Downfall, her last chance.

Seeking through her victim's eyes,
Cheeks blood-red,
Squirts of fear on the leaves,
Downfall, moments to go.

No guns, no knives, just a push,
It was no game,
It was just . . .
Knock, knock, she's dead!

Karly Dynes (10)
Cromer Junior School, Cromer

Destroying Me

Destroying me.
The world.
It hurts you know?
People driving cars.
All I can do is watch.
Wait,
For someone to notice.
I'm getting
Weaker and weaker.
Spinning,
Hoping
It will go.
My sky is choking.
It hurts.
My trees
Fading, fading,
Gone.
I wish I could forget,

Pollution!

Jordanna Yeo (10)
Cromer Junior School, Cromer

Lord Of The Rings

L oads of rings were forged that night
O rcs went out to fight
R ingwraiths ruled the dark days
D warves enchanted the mines

O ther men fought for their land
F ar from their homes to a dark place

T he Hobbits travelled to Mordor
H aving the ring to rule them all
E lrond, ruler of Rivendell

R eady to fight again
I senguard where Saruman's tower is
N azguls ruled Minas Morgul
G ollum led them to the eye
S tare at it if you dare.

Thomas Holroyd (11), Christopher Howe & Ieuan Simpkins
Cwmafan Junior School, Port Talbot

Planet Earth

E arth, blue and green
A wonderful planet
R ich in beauty
T eeming with life
H ome sweet home.

Aaron Diplock & Ross Smith (11)
Cwmafan Junior School, Port Talbot

The Demon Teacher

D evil man
E vil person
M ad flesh-eater
O n Earth but
N obody knows it

T eacher in disguise
E ating pupils young and old
A t the end of the day
C ursing the night that
H e ate you
E very parents' evening he
R ushes to get people in!

Tomas O'Leary, Jack Phillips (10)
& Kieran Hooper
Cwmafan Junior School, Port Talbot

Flumps

Flumps are slimy
Flumps have two eyes
Flumps have feelings
And go in disguise.

Flumps are very peaceful
Some are kind
But sometimes they
Are hard to find.

Caitlyn Thomas & Olivia Rees (10)
& Megan John (11)
Cwmafan Junior School, Port Talbot

Spooky

S pooky spiders creep through the house
P eople get scared, scream and shout
O ver the hill a witch cackles all night
O wls hoot, cause fright
K eep tucked up in bed
Y ou'll soon find out what spooks are about. *Boo! Argh!*

**Michaela Wood (10), Katie Murphy
& Emily Jones**
Cwmafan Junior School, Port Talbot

Animals

A nacondas curled up in the shade
N ine foals in the stable
I n the barn owls hoot
M ammals pouncing on their prey
A rmadillos gasping for water
L ions playing with their cubs
S now leopards cleaning their cubs.

Bethan Moore & Zoe Tanner
Cwmafan Junior School, Port Talbot

People

Old grumpy people need to eat
Especially 93-year-old Pete

When sporty people have a drink
All the water makes them think

Bad people kick with their feet
In the end they never get a treat

Lazy people in their beds
They're only fit in their heads!

Rhydian Bowden & Carwyn Davies
Cwmafan Junior School, Port Talbot

Minibeasts On The Move

Ladybirds flying in the air
Worms are wriggling everywhere
Woodlice living under rocks
Cuddling up in lots of moss.

Slimy slugs, there's an enemy coming,
Better watch out and try to be cunning.
Come on centipede, leave him alone,
Don't bug creatures, go on home.

Darcie Talbot & Sophie Slade (11)
Cwmafan Junior School, Port Talbot

The Marvellous Minibeasts

The busy bumblebee buzzes around
But it makes too much sound.
The lazy ladybird flies up high
Right up high in the sky.
The beautiful butterflies flutter into the wild
And they say, 'Flutter, flutter, goodbye.'

Denni-Tyla Bell (10), Molly Pickering & Chelsea Griffin
Cwmafan Junior School, Port Talbot

Mad Animals

Mad monkeys swinging in the trees
Happy hippos lying in the breeze.

Horses race, cheetahs chase, parrots sing,
Leopard spring.

Penguins sliding on the snow
Whales diving down below.

Jake Phillips & Emily Fisher (11)
Cwmafan Junior School, Port Talbot

Creepy-Crawlies In The Groove

Creepy-crawlies on the move
Everybody come and groove.

Parrots perch, leopards lurch
Ponies prance and dragonflies dance.

Ants dance with big, heavy pants
All day long the beat goes on.

Olivia Martin & Gethyn Hopson (10)
Cwmafan Junior School, Port Talbot

All Creatures On The Move

Centipedes always crawl and squirm,
While wiggly worms slither and turn.

Caterpillars jiggle slowly along,
While along the ground march the ants.

Beetles turn and jiggle their backs,
While butterflies float and relax.

Holly McNeil
Cwmafan Junior School, Port Talbot

Creature Feature

Creatures marching, having a ball,
As they perform their creepy crawl.

Frogs hopping, often stopping,
Grasshoppers body-popping.

Slithering snakes, sliding fast,
As they do their jelly dance.

Spiders having tomato toppings,
They're watching Mary Poppins.

Thomas Ebley
Cwmafan Junior School, Port Talbot

Trees

Trees are lovely
Trees are fine
Trees have got nice long vines
That anyone can climb.

Trees help us breathe
Trees have lovely leaves
In autumn leaves fall from trees
And we wouldn't breathe without trees.

**Thomas Holroyd, Christopher Howe
& Ieuan Simpkins**
Cwmafan Junior School, Port Talbot

Mad Animals

Mad monkeys swinging in the trees,
Happy hippos lying in the breeze

Horses race, cheetahs chase,
Parrots sing, leopards spring

Penguins sliding on the snow,
Whales diving down below

So many animals to be told
Some in the hot and some in the cold.

Demi Davies
Cwmafan Junior School, Port Talbot

Friendship

Friendship smells like violets
Friendship looks like a happy place
Friendship feels like a soft bunny
Friendship tastes like a chocolate bar
Friendship sounds like children screaming with happiness
Friendship is good for you and me!

Elliott Morgan (9)
Dunchurch Junior School, Dunchurch

Autumn Harvest

I can see old, brown leaves,
Acrobatically dancing from the tree.

I can hear the chirping of birds,
Eagerly flying to their nests.

I can smell the damp of the leaves,
That have piled proudly.

I can feel the cold,
So bitterly frozen.

I can taste the rosy-red apple,
I picked freshly this morning.

Autumn is like that,
Quiet and beautiful.

Harvest is coming,
There's no doubt about it.

I can see combine harvesters,
Scooping up the corn.

I can hear the wind,
Whistling through my ears.

I can smell the freshly picked vegetables,
About to be eaten for lunch.

I can feel the rough corn,
As I run through the cornfields.

I can taste fresh bread,
Made yesterday with my own hands.

Autumn is like that,
Quiet and beautiful.

Harvest is coming,
There's no doubt about it.

Jake Menesse (11)
Dunchurch Junior School, Dunchurch

Fireworks At The Bonfire

Flames crackling and jumping with joy
As they burn the dummy, Guy Fawkes;
Everyone turns round to face the colours of the fireworks . . .

Russet, crimson, sienna, maroon, scarlet,
Burgundy, flame and sea-green,
All bursting into view as the works, a masterpiece,
Are set off.

For a few minutes, the fireworks have been going,
But now they settle down for a little break,
Before they start again.

All the colours of the rainbow come back
As there are more expertly lit,
For they have started rushing up,
Catherine wheels, rockets, many more.

Children's hands are waving about excitedly
As they are being brought sparklers by their parents.
The sweet seller is also running around,
Worn out by his job.

Suddenly, all the deafening screams are gone
As loud stamps are heard,
As everyone turns round to face the bonfire again.

Guy is still in the heart of the flames,
Becoming ashes by the second,
Like all the other guys before him
That have faced the torture.

Erin Bashford (10)
Dunchurch Junior School, Dunchurch

Autumn Days

I can see
I can see the crimson apples blushing in the autumn days,
The golden, crisp leaves dancing and twirling to the ground,
Shiny conkers hatching out of their prickly homes.

I can hear
I can hear the sound of leaves whistling in the breeze,
The wind blowing through the oak trees,
Birds cheeping in the clear blue sky.

I can feel
I can feel the autumn air blowing onto my face,
Orange leaves falling gently onto my head,
The morning dew falling from above me.

I can smell
I can smell autumn air all around me,
Juicy fruits growing in the trees,
Sheaves of corn being picked from the fields.

I can taste
I can taste the sweet blackberries freshly picked,
Purple plums melting in my mouth,
Milk running down my throat.

Amy Thomas (10)
Dunchurch Junior School, Dunchurch

Best Friends

A best friend is someone who keeps a secret
And plays with you, who makes you laugh
And puts a smile on your face

A best friend is always a good friend to you
And you will always be a good friend to them

When you are in trouble they will help you
Even if they're far away from you.

Dan Hyslop (9)
Dunchurch Junior School, Dunchurch

Autumn Days

I can see the colourful leaves floating in the misty air,
I can see the birds flying round in circles,
I can see the bushes swaying in the wind.

I can hear the birds tweeting as they greet their friends,
I can hear the leaves rustling down to the ground,
I can hear the berries dropping off the bushes
And plopping to the ground.

I can smell the sweet smell of sour oranges,
I can smell the tangy apples that are on the trees,
I can smell the lemons splitting as the scented smell forms.

I can feel the rough, brown bark as it turns out its prickles,
I can feel the prickly shell as I get a conker out of it,
I can feel the leaves as I smoothly get hold of one
Before it drops.

I can taste the lush flavour of a blackberry as I bite into one,
I can taste my mother's pie as it falls into a deep sleep
Ready for me to eat it,
I can taste a fiery flame as I take a sip of my hot chocolate.

Sarah Jenkins (10)
Dunchurch Junior School, Dunchurch

Bonfire Night

Flames leap high, like fiery blades,
Slicing the pitch-black sky in two,
The poorly stuffed guy sitting limp on the chair.

My eyes start to water from the almighty light,
As do everybody's around me.
The logs burn grey, then black like ink.

White-hot sparks dance in the gentle breeze,
My dad's old clothes are turned into fireballs.
Eventually the light fades slowly and goes out.

Adam Cheney (10)
Dunchurch Junior School, Dunchurch

Bonfire Night

I can see fire blazing in the dark night,
Ruby-red flames flickering and dancing to a tune.

I can hear fireworks calling to each other,
A magical rainbow-scattered sky.

I can smell smoke rising to the fluffy clouds,
Smoky sparklers shine in the dark.

I can feel the warmth of the car as I watch fireworks zoom over
                                                                    my head,
A cosy hat and scarf to snuggle into.

I can taste hot dogs with strong mustard burning my mouth,
Butter melting as it touches my lips from the warm jacket potato
                                                                    in front of me.

Bonfire Night is finally here.

Kayleigh May Manning (10)
Dunchurch Junior School, Dunchurch

Bonfire Night

I can see the sparkling fireworks lighting up the lonely night sky
With their illuminating glow.

I can hear the booming and the shrieking
As the Lethal Tank shoots up into the black of the night.

I can smell hot dogs
Sizzling noisily in the pan.

I can feel the heat of the roaring bonfire guzzling up the timber,
Spitting out scorching hot sparks as it munches.

I can taste my dad's hot chilli con carne entering my mouth
And gently sliding down my throat and the black smoke in the air.

Florence Harris (10)
Dunchurch Junior School, Dunchurch

Friendship

Friendship is a feeling of happiness and love
As though you're in the air,
Friendship is what helps you live
Or your life is hard to bear.

Friendship can be difficult
It's better when it's easy,
If you find friendship hard
It will leave you feeling wheezy.

Friendship is great
Friendship is cool,
People will think
Without friends you're a fool!

Try and find a friend
That's kind and with no price,
It's not that hard, it's not that difficult
Friendship's prettier than sparkling ice.

Philip Dickinson (9)
Dunchurch Junior School, Dunchurch

Friendship

Friendship smells like chocolate cake
Friendship tastes of apple pie
Friendship looks like happy faces playing in the sun
Friendship feels like a butterfly in your body

Friendship doesn't taste like a rotten egg
Friendship doesn't smell like a dead man
Friendship doesn't look like a swamp
Friendship doesn't feel like death.

Corey Bevan (9)
Dunchurch Junior School, Dunchurch

Fantasy

The emerald-green of the dragon's eye flashed inquisitively
As its ebony-black tongue flicked out menacingly.

The wandering mounds of ground giants trudged along the forest,
Crushing everything in their path.

The unicorn's spear of ivory
Jutted from his silver forelock.

The burgundy and deep purple plumes
Sprouted from the phoenix's tail feathers.

The lustrous golden coat of the griffin
Shone spectacularly in the evening sun.

The snow-white wings of the Pegasus shone in the moonlight
Bigger than angels' wings
Shimmering like silver as it took off into the pitch-black night.

Imogen Fancourt (10)
Dunchurch Junior School, Dunchurch

Autumn

Leaves dancing gently to the floor
As the trees flick off their summer cloaks.

Flame flickering on the fire
As explosions go *crash* in the night.

Apples blushing in the sunlight
As they wait for autumn harvest.

The autumn breeze
Sweeping the gold and scarlet into huge mounds.

And last but not least
Birds flying to the tropics as winter closes in.

Sam Burn (10)
Dunchurch Junior School, Dunchurch

Bright Light

I was calling for my parents whilst I stumbled round,
Lost in the dark night.
All I could hear was the sound of pinewood burning away,
Crisping and sparkling in the bonfire's bright light.

I was crying and shouting for my parents or someone
To come and find me before the bonfire had burnt away
And before I was out of sight.
All I could hear was the sound of pinewood burning away,
Crisping and sparkling in the bonfire's bright light.

I needed help, I couldn't make it on my own, I was only 8 years old,
Maybe I could have, I just needed to fight, but hang on,
I could no longer hear the sound of pinewood burning away,
Crisping and sparkling in the bonfire's bright light.

It had all gone. I wasn't scared and I wasn't cold,
In fact I felt as if I wasn't outside.
Just then I could see the sun rising,
I started to walk towards it, then I bumped into a window.
Then the sun rose completely and I realised I was in my room
And it was only a dream.
I stared happily at the sun's bright light.

Sayla Maule (10)
Dunchurch Junior School, Dunchurch

Autumn Days

Golden, crimson leaves fluttering gently to the ground
And the huge ball of light playing hide-and-seek with the clouds.

The branches waving to one another
And beautiful birds singing a song in the breeze.

The smell of lush, fresh aromas from the colourful flowers
And the sweetness of the blackberries.

Apples blushing in the autumn sun
And the dandelions swaying to and fro.

Shanil Rathod (10)
Dunchurch Junior School, Dunchurch

Friendship

Friendship smells . . .
    like fresh roses in a bunch
    like gorgeous perfume
    like lilac and lavender

Friendship feels . . .
    like a soft, comforting blanket
    like stroking a fluffy bunny
    like a warm, gentle hug

Friendship tastes . . .
    like chocolate éclairs
    like strawberries and cream
    like lovely shortcake

Friendship sounds . . .
    like jolly laughter
    like giggling children
    like adults talking

Friendship looks . . .
    like big, happy smiles
    like your favourite holiday
    like posing models.

Carys Ireson (9)
Dunchurch Junior School, Dunchurch

Friendship

Friendship is letting someone under your coat
When it's raining.
Friendship is letting someone join in your game
When they do not have anyone to play with.
Friendship is helping someone
If they have fallen over.
Friendship is helping someone
If they are struggling with their work.

Alexander Holton (9)
Dunchurch Junior School, Dunchurch

Autumn

The ferocious wind sprints round the playground as if he is an
                                                                                           Olympic runner,
He pushes strongly anything in his path,
The fierce wind pushes and throws the small leaves around,
The strong wind wrestles the trees out of their feeble roots.

The old oak trees are listening to everything that is happening,
Another arm of the tree has fallen off and is falling to the
                                                                                             ground rapidly,
The trees moan and groan to the wind to make the wind stop,
More skin is falling off the trees and making them colder so
                                                                                                 they shiver.

The leaves are dancing in circles happily together,
The crispy brown leaves tiptoe, making hardly any noise,
Every leaf is screaming in horror as now they are getting bullied
                                                                                                by the wind,
The wind has now stopped and the leaves are still and calm,
Resting at the foot of the tree.

Luke Norman (10)
Dunchurch Junior School, Dunchurch

Friendship

F riendship is better than pure solid gold
R elationships help you in many ways
I can help people because I am a good friend
E veryone deserves a friend
N ever leave your best friend lonely
D eserve a friendship that will never end
S ecrets are kept private by friends
H aving a friendship can help you through life
I n a situation that you and a friend fall out, try to make up quickly
P lease help your best friend when they need you.

Harriet Smith (9)
Dunchurch Junior School, Dunchurch

Friendship

Friendship smells   like lovely roses
      .   like perfume
                      like gorgeous chicken

Friendship feels   like warm, comforting cuddles
                     like a soft, furry cushion
                     like a tummy full up with delicious food

Friendship tastes   like delightful chocolate
                     like toffee cake
                     like a scone with jam and cream

Friendship looks   like a famous film star
                     like a model
                     like the best thing in the world

Friendship sounds like children singing
                     like a teacher's helpful voice
                     like jolly laughter.

Ariane Turner (9)
Dunchurch Junior School, Dunchurch

Untitled

The crazy wind punches helpless old people to the stony ground.
It kicks innocent trees and robs them of their leaves.
The wild wind snatches roofs off houses.
The old oak tree punches back at the wind angrily.

He shivers madly as cold rain falls softly on his branches.
He moans sadly, 'Stop wind, stop blowing me over.'

The small leaves leap happily up in the air towards the sun,
They dance down silently and rest on the forest floor,
Then they sleep in the golden sunlight.

Declan Turnbull (10)
Dunchurch Junior School, Dunchurch

Autumn

Blitzen the wind pushed the people over when he sneezed,
He shouted at the trees and said, 'Fall over trees!'
He wrestled the trees and headbutted trees over,
He blew the market over like a tornado as he sneezed.

Comet the tree yawned tiredly in the cold, dingy morning,
He was fighting against the wind when suddenly a branch fell off,
His skin peeled off second by second and gradually he got colder,
He moaned at Blitzen and suddenly there was a thud, he had fallen
heavily to the ground.

The leaves danced and did pirouettes in the air,
They skipped merrily in a circle and sang, 'Hippety, hopperty, ho.'
They started to scream and run as the wind got stronger,
They started to fly in the air as the wind calmed down.
They floated down to the soft ground.

Oliver Smith (10)
Dunchurch Junior School, Dunchurch

Autumn

The crunchy, dark brown leaves dance happily and cheerfully together in the cold, blustery autumn morning.
The leaping wind throws the leaves around and wrestles and headbutts the tree to the ground.
The tree moans when the wind blows his leaves and snaps
and peels off his skin.
The leaves run, skip and scream while playing happily.
The wind sneezes and knocks over everything in its way.
The tree kicks and punches at the wind whilst he blows the leaves
off the trees.
The leaves blow everywhere, playing, yelling and jumping.
The wind dives at the trees and snaps all their branches.
The tree yells and calls, but the wind pushes.

Calum O'Keefe (10)
Dunchurch Junior School, Dunchurch

Autumn

Suddenly there was a bluster in the air,
The wind was feeling angry,
Then it shouted, 'I'm gonna get you!'
It shouted through the poor trees and the living plants,
It shouted through the cars as if it was in a trance,
The wind was indestructible.

The tree heard the wind coming and thought he'd better hide,
But couldn't find anything to hide behind.
Oh no, he thought as he waved to his friends,
But the wind sprang through the tree without a care.

The leaves got pushed off their tree by the wind,
No matter how hard they tried to hold on,
The leaves squealed, 'Help us! Save us!'
But the wind just intimidated them.
The leaves slowly danced to the ground,
It is as if they were hibernating through the winter months.

Josh Ireson (11)
Dunchurch Junior School, Dunchurch

Autumn

The wind talks to the little children apart from his blowing.
His name, William,
When he sneezes, his wind is really strong,
When he pushes, he knocks all the young children over.

Tayler shivers when he is cold,
Tayler yells to the leaves to come back when the wind blows.
The trees moan and groan at the wind when it forces them to fall off.
The trees break in the strong wind.

The leaves dance and prance in the wind,
The leaves do somersaults as they fall through the air,
The leaves scream as they fall down,
They cry as they leave the tree.

Lawrence Baker (10)
Dunchurch Junior School, Dunchurch

Autumn Days

The wind is strong,
It is a big, bad bully.
Trees beware,
Trees beware,
The wind is like a bear.
The cunning wind dives and fights angrily,
It shouts out at the sun when it gets hot,
Its name is Tornadus.

The tree moans and groans at the wind,
It shivers in the cold, freezing wind,
Its bendy branches smack the wind aggressively.

The leaves dance,
They tiptoe at night,
They whisper to each other,
They are scared of the dark.

Shane Jenkinson (11)
Dunchurch Junior School, Dunchurch

Autumn

Whippy the wind blew his bulging cheeks,
He gave a huge bellow and the roof blew off,
Viciously wrestling an enormous oak tree to the ground.

Twisting and turning in an angry rage,
Angrily it slapped itself with its spindly arms,
The tree shivered and all its leaves fell off.

The leaves danced around the oak tree,
Their dark, veiny mouths whispered secrets to the trees,
Like ballerinas they pirouetted around the tree.

Matthew Rush (10)
Dunchurch Junior School, Dunchurch

Autumn

The wind blows over the busy market place as the children chatter.
It shivers and it spins and twirls around the market,
As if it is an icy, cold tornado.
The wind sneezes over the town.
The strong wind headbutts the bark on trees and knocks them over.

The thin, cold, stick twigs are chattering in the freezing cold,
shivery wind
As it waves by the warm house down the street.
The tree is proud, it stares at the horror coming towards it.
As the tree's branches and bark come off, the wind rushes around it,
Leaving it cold and bare.

The leaves dance in the stormy, rainy, wet night,
The wind makes the leaves dance and sing, 'Hoorah, hoorah!'
But as the crisp morning air comes, the tree goes to sleep.
The wind leaves tiredly, the leaves sleep and the trees rest.

Jamie Ross (10)
Dunchurch Junior School, Dunchurch

Friendship

Friendship tastes like freshly baked chocolate chip cookies
Just after leaving the oven.
Friendship looks like a cheeky smile on a glowing face.
Friendship smells like bacon, sausage and eggs
First thing in the morning.
Friendship feels like holding hands with your best friend.

Ross Carlton (9)
Dunchurch Junior School, Dunchurch

Autumn

The ferocious wind runs around the crowded playground,
As he destroys the trees and snatches the leaves off the branches,
He is scary.
The wind commands the leaves to run away.
'Go forth,' he shouts.
He bullies the children that are not wearing a coat.

The trees moan, 'Come back to me golden-brown, happy leaves,
I need some warmth.'
All of the big, worn out oak trees can smell the fuel
Of the smelly chainsaw coming to get him on a crisp October morning.
His biggest limb starts to crack and then *crash!*
It hits the ground with an almighty thump.

The leaves play happily a game of tig around the trees,
They dance and pirouette to a wise tune.
The leaves sing with joy as they tiptoe on the fresh autumn grass,
They go to sleep when the wind dies down, resting at the foot of
                                                    the tree.

Alex Smith (10)
Dunchurch Junior School, Dunchurch

Friendship

Friendship smells like baking cakes
Friendship looks like people playing
Friendship sounds like laughter and cheering
Friendship tastes of sugary sweets dancing in your mouth
Friendship reminds me of happiness in your head.

Friendship is *amazing!*

Ben Malin (9)
Dunchurch Junior School, Dunchurch

Autumn

The fierce wind whistles, bringing the leaves off their feet.
'Get out of my way!' bellows the wind.
The wind stares at people and trees with his big, beady eyes
And shouts at the leaves with his big, wide mouth.
He is scary.
The wind smells all the fresh autumn leaves and all the bark on
                                                            the trees.
When the leaves hear the wind, they try not to look and they shiver.

The leaves hear the wind. They twizzle around in the sky.
The leaves shiver as their skin peels off.
'Yippee, we are out of our summer clothes and into our winter
                                              clothes,' shout the leaves.
The leaves pirouette around and around in circles.
Tiptoe, tiptoe go the leaves as they fall to the ground.

The trees wave around in the storm.
'Ouch!' shouts the tree, 'My branch has fallen off!'
The tree fights with the rainy, wet storm as his leaves fall off.
'Oh, give me back my leaves, I am freezing,' shouts the tree
As he stands shivering on the cold autumn grass.

Hannah Downes (10)
Dunchurch Junior School, Dunchurch

Friendship

Friendship looks like a group of friends
Friendship tastes like a Galaxy bar
Friendship sounds like people saying you can play tag to their
                                                            best friend
Friendship feels like my great dog, Monty
Friendship smells like a bunch of red roses.

Matthew Dunkley (9)
Dunchurch Junior School, Dunchurch

Autumn

The wind will whistle like a kettle boiling and steaming,
He will push at people like a big, scary, mean bully.
The wind will destroy the park like a giant, ferocious beast,
He will shout at the trees with a big low voice.
The wind will blow people over when he sneezes,
He will stare at people when he is angry and will be as mean as
he can.
He will hear the leaves even when they tiptoe.

The tree will wave at everyone,
He will moan like a baby.
The tree will shout at everyone if he wants his leaves back,
He might break his branches in the wind as his arms are blown away.
The tree will try to fight the wind,
He will bend his body to try and fix his branch.
The tree will groan at everyone if he loses the fight.

The leaves will dance around with the wind,
Leaves will be jumping around in circles.
The leaves might fall in a river and float away,
Leaves will play tig or chase when it is autumn.
The leaves will tiptoe to try and get away,
Leaves will be scared and very upset.

Then the wispy wind will die and the leaves will fall down.

Michelle Murdoch (10)
Dunchurch Junior School, Dunchurch

Friendship

Friendship looks like children playing
Friendship smells like a bunch of roses
Friendship tastes like chocolate
Friendship sounds like children laughing
Friendship feels like soft silk.

Ashley Fiedler (9)
Dunchurch Junior School, Dunchurch

Autumn

As the wind whistles, he gets more vicious every time
And gets closer and starts a fight.
He tries to wrestle with the trees and he chases the leaves.
'Blow over!' bellows the wind
And he starts to headbutt the really weak trees.
The wind sneezes and all the germs push over the leaves
And they all fall to the ground.

The trees are so weak that one suddenly loses an arm
And it blames the wind.
The other trees are trying to fight with the wind,
But they can't reach him.
As for the ones that are standing and not giving up,
The wind starts to chase them.
They play under his feet, having a laugh and a joke.

The leaves hate being chased so they have an idea
To go different ways so he won't be able to know where to go.
But the wind finds a way and he catches most of them,
(But not all of them).
The leaves dance joyfully on their tiptoes
Upon the crisp, autumn grass.
As the dark autumn night draws in,
The leaves go to sleep at the trees' feet.

Lauren Peel (10)
Dunchurch Junior School, Dunchurch

Friendship

Friendship smells like melted chocolate
Friendship feels like soft, warm blankets
Friendship sounds like lots of friends laughing
Friendship looks like a sunny day at the beach
Friendship tastes like milk chocolate essence
Friendship is fabulous!

Marcus Coles (9)
Dunchurch Junior School, Dunchurch

Autumn

Larry the leaf plays with the other bright yellow and orange leaves
As they dance slowly off the tree.
Larry the leaf trips over off the tree and slowly glides to the ground.
Larry the leaf never rushes, he always takes his time.
Larry the leaf wobbles one day and stays on by a thread
And the next day he falls.

Thomas the tree fights with the wind and tries to defend himself.
Thomas the tree's poor, helpless skin falls off bit by bit each day,
Leaving him bare.
Thomas the tree just sits there all day thinking,
Listening to your conversation.
Thomas the tree breaks his body parts in the vicious wind.

Wally the wind wrestles the trees and roars at them.
Wally the wind smacks down all the trees with his deadly powers.
Wally the wind knocks off all the leaves from the tree.
Wally the wind whistles and shouts and when he sneezes,
He knocks all the weak people over.

Thomas Oglethorpe (10)
Dunchurch Junior School, Dunchurch

Friendship

Friendship smells like chocolate cake
Friendship looks like a smile on your face
Friendship tastes like my favourite tea
Friendship is you and me.

Luke Menesse (9)
Dunchurch Junior School, Dunchurch

Autumn

The big, mighty wind was blowing around the dark forest,
Hitting the trees.
Then a big gust came along and pushed over some of the trees.
Next he stepped to the biggest, strongest tree in the whole forest.
He started sneezing round the roots of the tree to pull it down,
Then the tree started fighting back.

The wind viciously pulled the tree right down to his knees,
Then he swung with a right hook at the wind,
So the wind and the leaves started laughing at him.
Afterwards, the tree punched the wind again and he just missed,
But the leaves giggled more than ever!
The leaves were jumping and running
And catching each other around the forest.
Next the tree shouted, 'Come back, leaves!'
Then the tree fell over onto his knees on the ground
And the leaves went off to sleep.

Rhys Warren (10)
Dunchurch Junior School, Dunchurch

Autumn

I can see golden leaves floating around me
And farmers gathering in their crops.

I can smell juicy fruits growing in the trees
And delicious vegetables in the fields.

I can hear birds calling to each other
And the wind whistling.

I can taste rosy-red apples from the trees
And juicy, freshly picked berries from the bushes.

I can feel leaves falling onto my head
And the morning dew drifting from the trees above me.

Katie Mackenzie (10)
Dunchurch Junior School, Dunchurch

Autumn Days

The wind pushes the trees about on the cold September morning,
It fights, pushes and pulls at every tree in the woods and forest.
It sneezes hard and knocks all the young children down,
It leaps about the garden, chasing everything.

Tom shivers in the strong wind as bark peels off his skin.
His worn out branches fall off and crash when they hit the ground
And land in the different coloured leaves.
He shouts at the wind, 'Leave me alone!'
The leaves fall off the tree, bare, cold and shivering.

The leaves dance around in circles and do pirouettes in the air.
They tiptoe up and down the autumn-covered garden,
They fly in cold, crisp air and whisper to each other,
They skip together in the long wet grass.

Courtney Phillips (10)
Dunchurch Junior School, Dunchurch

Friendship

F riendship comes in all shapes and sizes
R emember that friendships are worth more than gold
I have a friend to rely on
E ven if you don't have a best friend, you should have a friend
N eed a friend
D on't disagree with all your buddies
S hould give respect
H e or she should have a friend
I n friendship all of us are happy
P lease accept people.

Ruby Hartland (9)
Dunchurch Junior School, Dunchurch

Autumn

The ferocious wind, Gusty, was angry and sprinted across the forest, waking up all the animals and nature.
He was shouting in his furious voice, 'I'm going to get you trees and leaves.'
He sprinted once more across the oak forest, headbutting three trees.
He dived down for a fight with the trees and leaves, planning to destroy them.

He shot his thunder down with a huge roar.
Oaky, one of the only surviving trees, broke his arm and it fell to the floor with a smack.
His skin started to peel off which made him cold.
He tried to defend himself by swinging his arms at the wind, Gusty, but he was too fast.
He waved at a warm cottage in the woods.
The wind thrashed off the leaves on Oaky's arms, this made him shiver.
He was freezing cold. 'Give back my leaves,' he said quietly.

The wind had another uproar and the leaves started dancing in the air.
'Hip hip hooray, it's a wonderful day!' they were singing joyfully.
They were orange and brown and lots of other colours too, they had changed to their autumn clothes.
Gusty died a death and left the leaves asleep at the foot of the tree.

Joe Fletcher (11)
Dunchurch Junior School, Dunchurch

Friendship

Friendship smells like a freshly made cookie.
Friendship looks like fun.
Friendship sounds like laughing.
Friendship feels good and makes you happy.

Joshua Whitington (9)
Dunchurch Junior School, Dunchurch

Autumn

The wind fights like a warrior, fiercely trying to blow off all the
    helpless, whispering leaves.
He punches everything in his path and he throws everything that
    he pulls up out of the ground.
The wind will snatch everyone's belongings and will snatch the
    tree's leaves.
He will dive and scream when he is angry, as he can get very cross.
The tree's leaves will have come off, leaving the tree's
    teeth chattering.
He waves happily at people below and brightens their day.
He unfortunately loses a limb and it comes crashing to the ground.
The tree is yelling for help, but no one comes.
The leaves dance happily around in circles.
The leaves are pirouetting around the tree with glee,
They are happily playing, running up and down the tree.
The leaves can tiptoe around without making a noise.

Lauren Love (10)
Dunchurch Junior School, Dunchurch

Autumn Days

I can see crimson leaves floating to the ground,
Children playing on their bikes laughing all around.

I can hear rustling branches singing a graceful song,
Birds chirping away and the wedding bell goes *dong*.

I can feel frost landing on my eyelashes,
Prickly needles from the pine tree in little lashes.

I can taste blueberries from the blueberry bush,
As they crush in my mouth they taste so lush.

I can smell apple pies burning from the house,
I look around and what do I see?
Oh no, there's a mouse!

Imogen Slinn (10)
Dunchurch Junior School, Dunchurch

Autumn

Swirling leaves,
Waltzing with the wind.
A russet conker
Gently being shaken out of its branch.
Shiny rain droplets,
Imprinting ripples in the reflective pond.
Apples blushing,
In the early evening sun.

Crunchy leaves,
Coloured crimson, gold and burgundy.
The chill,
Freezing everything in its path.
The emerald-green grass,
Its dew sparkling in the sun
And the wind,
Howling and screeching at anything it
Desires.

Tom Crathorne (11)
Dunchurch Junior School, Dunchurch

Friendship

Friendship smells like sweet vanilla
Friendship smells like red roses

Friendship looks like a smile
Friendship looks like fun

Friendship feels like happiness
Friendship feels like a soft bed

Friendship sounds like laughter
Friendship sounds like secrets

Friendship tastes like sugar
Friendship tastes like marshmallows.

Eve Palmer (10)
Dunchurch Junior School, Dunchurch

An Autumn Day

A new autumn day is dawning
And the birds are singing their morning song,
Tweeting in the trees,
The birds awaken the sky.

Mahogany leaves flutter gracefully to the ground,
The colourful leaves are dancing graciously,
As the oak tree shakes off its golden coat,
The wind catches the leaves' every move.

The combine harvester is roaring its way through the wheat fields,
The frightened wheat surrenders to the almighty machine,
Crops are scorched by the burning sun,
But saved by the harvesting.

The wind rustles the leaves loudly,
Crunching and cracking under my feet,
The end of the day has come.

The rainbow-washed sky shines light to the wondering world,
As I lie in the light, I gaze upon the setting sun,
As the end has come.

Emily March (10)
Dunchurch Junior School, Dunchurch

Good Friends

Good friends put a smile on your face
And make sure you never frown

Good friends always play with you
And make sure you're never alone

Good friends help you with your work
And help you when you're stuck

Good friends are worth keeping.

Richard Massie (9)
Dunchurch Junior School, Dunchurch

Autumn Days

On autumn days the dainty leaves do the waltz in the gentle breeze,
Gorgeous sweet fragrance from the freshly picked fruit
Lingers in the air.
As I walk through the fields,
Soft sheaths of corn gently brush my legs,
When the ancient trees brush off their summer clothing,
It elegantly does the samba to the ground.

On autumn days the pleasant sunshine smiles down
On the folk of Britain,
The fearful, glistening corn tries to dodge the roaring monster
That is rapidly racing towards them.

On autumn days I can smell the familiar odour of mahogany bark,
And the lovely scent of harvested wheat.
I can see glittering, red apples blushing in the sunlight
And smooth, golden corn bowing down with terrible fright.

On autumn days I can taste silver, cold raindrops
Landing on my tongue,
Sweet, ripe berries squelching in my mouth,
Local vegetables on my plate covered in gravy
And the warm loaf made from the first sheaf of wheat.

On autumn days I can feel golden leaves blowing past my ankles,
Rosy-red fruits touching my lips,
And the cold chill of the shivering wind
As I wrap up warmly in my winter clothing.

Samantha Townsend (10)
Dunchurch Junior School, Dunchurch

Friendship

Friendship smells like scented sweets,
Friendship tastes like chocolate cake,
Friendship feels like cuddly toys,
Friendship looks like red roses,
And that's what friends are like.

Samuel Barnes (9)
Dunchurch Junior School, Dunchurch

Autumn

I can see
The leaves
They're jumping off the trees
Then they are floating to the ground

I can hear
I can hear birds chirping and singing
The ripple of corn
The wind whistling through the trees

Smell
The waft of cooking
Drifting out of windows

Taste
I can taste apple pie
Lingering in my mouth

Touch
I can feel the
Roughness of the corn
As I run through the field.

Jo-Jo Pendlebury (10)
Dunchurch Junior School, Dunchurch

Friendships

Friendships can relieve your worries in many ways,
They can also make you happy.

Every person needs a good friend
To have a great big shoulder to cry on.

If you do not have a friend,
You can be very lonely.

Friends can help you
With terrible worries.

Sara Pawsey (9)
Dunchurch Junior School, Dunchurch

Autumn

Billy is the most vicious wind ever in autumn.
Billy loves to pick a fight with trees and if he's got enough energy,
He'll wrestle and headbutt the leaves.
He'll fight no matter what the cause and his favourite thing
Is to punish and enslave.

Mick is a snapping good tree.
He loves his leaves more than anything and he always says,
'They grow up so fast!'
Every autumn he will hug his leaves and will try to lift them back up
Onto his bending branches.

The reddish-brown leaves are the most playful
And they're always full of energy.
They are always dancing and being happy,
They also love Mick very much.
Billy loves smacking the leaves around and they always call for help,
But it does no good.

Jake Lewis (10)
Dunchurch Junior School, Dunchurch

Autumn

The howling wind bellowed at all the people beneath it, with an
                                                    angry roar.
Like a bully, it violently thrashed at the trees, trying to destroy them.
It dived down fiercely like a vulture, headbutted the battered old oak
                                            and threw it to its knees.

The trees whistled and moaned as the wind punched and hit them.
Their weak arms were snapped by the wind's crushing blows.
They shivered all the way to their feet with every powerful gust
                                                    of wind.

The crunchy, dark brown leaves danced happily and cheerfully
                    together in the cold, blustery autumn morning.
The golden leaves skipped on the smooth ground.
They cried mournfully as they were forced to leave their tree mother.

Alex James Smith (10)
Dunchurch Junior School, Dunchurch

Autumn

Willy the wind sneezes because he has a cold
And blows the innocent people helplessly around the town.
Willy shouts down to people that he is in control.
He snatches trees and throws them like they're his javelin.
Willy wrestles with the helpless trees, throwing them out of the way.

Thomas the tree gets hit and battered by the wind.
He helplessly watches as his arm falls to the ground.
His leaves are flying all around him.
He yells, 'Go away, wind!'

Luke the leaf glides round happily like he is at the fair.
He can hear the whistling of the wind.
Him and the other leaves are whispering to each other.
The wind suddenly drops all the leaves at the tree's feet.

Harry Dibsdale (10)
Dunchurch Junior School, Dunchurch

Autumn

Paul moans in the headbutting wind.
Paul's brown, scaly skin peels off in the vicious wind.
Paul watches the leaves pirouette round in a circle.
He waves to the people as they pass by.
Paul sadly falls over in the whistly winds.

Sally and her friends dance happily in the wind.
Sally cries sadly as her brothers and sisters flutter away.
She tiptoes quietly around the tree's trunk.
She sings beautifully when the storm calms down.
Sally wobbles around when she is very dizzy.

Eddie bullies the scared leaves and trees.
Eddie shouts violently to be bold.
Eddie fights with the east wind,
He throws people violently to the ground.
Eddie commands to be the great king.

Chelsea Lloyd (10)
Dunchurch Junior School, Dunchurch

The New Shoe

I am brand new,
No one has even worn me,
I'm orange,
Female and have a lovely wedge,
I have loads of friends,
But only because I'm pretty.

There's a really good-looking woman in the shop,
The shopkeeper's reaching for the window,
She's pinching my straps,
The wonderful woman is trying me on,
I'm moving house!

She wears me every day now,
She adores me, I'm so happy,
When we go to town, all her friends say
How beautiful I look,
But,
It's starting to rain,
I'll be ruined,
Doesn't matter, we're inside now, *phew!*

Isabel Sharratt (10)
Dunchurch Junior School, Dunchurch

Bonfire Night

The night begins with a coloured display,
Lighting up the lonely, black sky.
Twists and turns of a painted air,
The broken particles of the light falling on my face.

The fire is lit below an old, ragged man,
Burning golden, crimson and burgundy.
As the fire swallows the threadbare doll,
The fire burns down to ash.

Jessica Armitage (10)
Dunchurch Junior School, Dunchurch

Bonfire Night

I can see sparks flashing in the night light,
I can see the fireworks zooming up in the sky
And then exploding into the most fascinating colours.

I can hear the sparklers crackling in my ear,
I can hear the children playing around the bonfire.

I can smell the smoke coming off the bonfire
And hot dogs freshly off the BBQ.
I can smell the fireworks as they come charging down from the sky.

I can taste the hot dogs as they touch my mouth
And the Coke as I gulp it down.
I can taste the chips as I dip them into the ketchup.

I can feel the leather gloves as I hold the sparkler
And as I hold the burger to my mouth.
I can feel the wood slip through my fingers as I throw it on the fire.

Ben Williamson (11)
Dunchurch Junior School, Dunchurch

Bonfire Night

I can see the dancing fireworks
Sparkling elegantly in the dark night sky.

I can hear the amazement of people
And the bangs and booms of the shimmering fireworks.

I can smell the hot dogs steaming
From their griddle pan
The scent of food tormenting me.

I can feel the heat of the burning fire
And the cold, bitter air around me.

I can taste the fast food from brightly lit stalls
And the thick black smoke in the air.

Eleanor Jones (10)
Dunchurch Junior School, Dunchurch

My Autumn Senses

I can see,
Golden leaves waltzing down to the ground,
The birds shooting across the sky like jets in the light
In the sunflower's head,
Children running through domes of settled leaves
And trees swaying in the gentle breeze.

I can hear,
The rustling of the branches in the cold breeze,
The wind whistling as if it's trying to round up a herd of sheep,
Children laughing as they ride their bikes down the city park path,
Birds in the choir on a branch in the light-loving forest.

I can smell,
The freshly cut corn from the protective field,
The fuel from the combine harvester's long day of never-ending work,
The apple pie that the children made with their parents,
The harvest roast cooking from the kitchen.

I can feel,
The first frost on the bark of the tree
When I go to hug it to see how tall it is,
The dirt of the newborn carrots as I pick them for harvest,
The prickly thorns on the conker's bed,
Crusty bread as I crunch it in my wet mouth
And it tickles my taste buds.

I can taste,
The bunches of berries that nature has grown to keep me running,
The apple pie that my mother worked hard on all day,
I've finally had a piece,
Gingerbread men crumble in my mouth,
Scarlet-red apples now lush and golden.

Shannon Moor (10)
Dunchurch Junior School, Dunchurch

Autumn Times

I can see
Mahogany conkers creeping out of their shells
And rosy-red apples falling out of the trees,
Khaki leaves waltzing around.

I can smell
Juicy fruits being gathered up by farmers
Pretty little daisies growing older by the minute
And freshly cut corn sheaves
Huddling together
For the roaring harvester is racing after them.

I can hear
Birds perched on branches
Singing in the early mornings.
The almighty, roaring monster
Loudly approaching the petite, timid corn sheaves.

I can feel
A gentle breeze calling to the dainty leaves
To partner him in a dance,
The crispy feeling of the branches
Shaking off their dark, russet leaves,
Leaving them to crisp and freeze
In the winter.

I can taste
Crunchy carrots, cold in my mouth
And the smooth taste of red berries
Grown on a bush
And picked fresh this morning.

Jessica Thompson (10)
Dunchurch Junior School, Dunchurch

Autumn And Winter Days

I can feel the frozen branches as they wrap around me
In the gloomy, dark forest,
The frosty grass
Crunching underneath my cold feet,
Rough leaves quietly and gracefully
Waltzing down to the damp ground,
Bushes of scarlet leaves
As I walk along the gravel path,
The light breeze swishing and swaying around me
As I walk through a huge crowd of people,
The wind whistling through the bare branches,
I can see grey clouds overlapping blue clouds
As I look across the murky sky,
Rosy-red apples blushing brightly
Getting ready for the delicious apple pie,
Cars warming up as the morning sun
Slowly appears in the distance,
Crimson berries tickling my taste buds
As I munch them slowly, *yum,*
What a fantastic but cold autumn
This is going to be!

Ellie Smith (10)
Dunchurch Junior School, Dunchurch

Autumn Days

I can see
Leaves waltzing in the breeze,
Shades of scarlet, gold and mahogany all around me,
Branches waving as if they can feel the joy in my heart.

I can hear
Birds chattering amongst themselves,
Wind whistling through the trees,
Leaves whispering to one another.

I can taste
Gooseberries pinching my tongue,
Pear juice dribbling down my chin,
Bread and marmalade moistening my mouth.

I can smell
Sheaves of corn waiting to be knocked out by the roaring lion,
Rosy-red apples clinging onto the branches in the breeze,
The sweetness of fruits hanging about waiting to be picked.

I can feel
Wind wrapping itself around me,
Leaves stroking my ankles,
A cold chill in the air as a sign of winter arriving.

Gemma Trodd (10)
Dunchurch Junior School, Dunchurch

Autumn Leaves

Crimson, gold and russet,
Trees gently shaking off their scarlet cloaks,
The last of the emerald fading away.

Leaves dancing gracefully in the wind,
All sizes of leaves dappled with many colours,
Wind sweeping leaves into piles.

Leaves that look like painted pictures,
They twirl and sway in the breeze,
Sienna, maroon and burgundy.

Isabel Parsons (10)
Dunchurch Junior School, Dunchurch

Mine Disaster

I can see coal burning,
Fire blazing,
And the dark mine lighting up with
Scarlet and crimson colours.

I can hear boys screaming,
Pit ponies neighing
And the explosions, bangs
And slamming of doors.

I can smell smoke rising
And gases travelling through the air
At a very fast pace.

I can feel the heat from the fire
And children screaming,
Coal crumbling beneath my feet.

Alice Hargreaves (10)
Dunchurch Junior School, Dunchurch

The Five Senses On Bonfire Night

I can see sparks of orange, red and white
And fireworks shooting into the air.

I can hear fireworks as they explode
And children playing round the bonfire.

I can smell gunpowder from the fireworks
And hot dogs from the barbecue.

I can feel the warm air
And my gloves keeping me warm.

I can taste the musty air
And a burger as I eat it.

Woody Woodbridge (10)
Dunchurch Junior School, Dunchurch

My Magic Box
(Based on 'Magic Box' by Kit Wright)

I will put in the box . . .

An angry toucan being shot
Flying up into the sky wounded.
Jealous Joe playing football
But losing.
A witch on a skateboard
And a boy on a broomstick.

My box is fashioned from . . .

Clouds and gold and stars
With trains on the lid
And water in the corners.

Courtney Cowens (8)
Millfield Primary School, North Walsham

My Magic Box
(Based on 'Magic Box' by Kit Wright)

I will put in the box . . .

All the shiny money rattling in a pocket.
An orange, pretty cloud floating in the sunset.
A dog that is brown and loud and barking.
A BMW that goes super fast at racing.
Speeding down the street in a BMW, a city with no laws.

My box is fashioned from . . .

Gold, silver and glass
With crystal on the lid
And bronze in the corners.

James Turner (8)
Millfield Primary School, North Walsham

My Magic Box
(Based on 'Magic Box' by Kit Wright)

I will put in my box . . .

A huge, scary, green dinosaur,
A fat snowman with a giant belly,
The freezing sun and a dry lake.

My box is fashioned from . . .

Silver and gold and bronze,
With pink on the lid
And a bow in the corners.

Hannah Richards (8)
Millfield Primary School, North Walsham

My Magic Box
(Based on 'Magic Box' by Kit Wright)

I will put into my box . . .

A Ferrari that roars louder than a lion,
All the solid gold in the galaxy,
Sitting in a giant, solid metal safe.
Burger King that gives away free burgers to the world.

I will fashion my box from . . .

Hot, burning lava with little volcanoes on the lid
And fire flowing down the sides.

James Maisner (8)
Millfield Primary School, North Walsham

My Magic Box
(Based on 'Magic Box' by Kit Wright)

I will put in the box . . .

A snowman frozen solid
Like a planet made of snow.

I will put in the box . . .

A peaceful snowball fight
And a peaceful island.

My box is fashioned from . . .

Gold and steel and wood
With stars on the lid.
The corners are made of ice.

Luke Watling (8)
Millfield Primary School, North Walsham

Happiness

Happiness is yellow, like a beautiful twinkling diamond.
It sounds like a wonderful dove singing for her graceful mother.
It looks like a beautiful rose rising to Heaven.
It tastes like a freshly baked cake.
It smells like the sweetest candy in the world.
It feels like a happy, smiley face.
It reminds me of my happy, sweet family.

Jemaica Bermas (8)
Our Lady & St Michael's RC Primary School, Abergavenny

Fear

It sounds like a strong star
It tastes like a salty tear
It smells like a team of tennis players
It feels like a fearless dragon
It reminds me of my first day in school.

Jojo Arthur (8)
Our Lady & St Michael's RC Primary School, Abergavenny

Love . . .

Love is red like a heart.
It looks like a hurricane.
It smells like a sweet smell of a brand new day.
It feels like you're in a swimming pool.
It reminds me of my lovely friends.

Oliver Tod (8)
Our Lady & St Michael's RC Primary School, Abergavenny

A Wizard Is . . .

Splendid like the royal family of kings,
Noble like a knight when he fights,
Kind like a lovely angel who works for God,
Armed with magical powers that are dangerous,
Stunning on the inside, but ugly on the outside.

Rosanna Williams (8)
Our Lady & St Michael's RC Primary School, Abergavenny

A Wizard Is . . .

Intelligent like a calculator,
So powerful he can explode,
Brave like a knight in shining armour,
Detailed like a 100-year-old warrior,
Crazy like an insane wet barrel of monkeys,
Funny like a magical comedy show,
Covered with magical, sparkly dust.

Moira Taylor (8)
Our Lady & St Michael's RC Primary School, Abergavenny

Nervous

It smells like old socks.
It looks like a pig.
It feels like slime.
It sounds like a strangled cat.
It reminds me of my brothers.

Jacob Pearl (9)
Our Lady & St Michael's RC Primary School, Abergavenny

Nervous

Nervous is blue, like the waving blue sea.
It tastes like freshly baked blueberry pie.
It sounds like bluebells ringing in my ear.
It looks like a full bush of blueberries waiting to be picked.
It smells of fresh blue roses that someone has picked because
they love you.
It feels like someone is picking on you, but you don't know who it is.
It reminds me of messing up really badly.

Ella Walsh (8)
Our Lady & St Michael's RC Primary School, Abergavenny

Tired

Tired is orange, like a soft and comfy bed.
It sounds like a calm and peaceful sound.
The snoring sounds loud, like birds singing in the sky.
It feels like a comfy and warm feeling that you've never felt before.
It smells like a freshly baked cake.
It reminds me of having relaxation.

Morgan Lewis (8)
Our Lady & St Michael's RC Primary School, Abergavenny

A Wizard Is . . .

Extremely strange, like the dark side of the moon,
Is wicked like a mysterious, open ocean,
Is mad like the roaring river,
Is unknown like a curious word,
Extremely powerful like lightning,
Is evil like the powerful Devil.

Talitha Morrish (8)
Our Lady & St Michael's RC Primary School, Abergavenny

Anger

Anger is red, like a red devil from Hell ready to assassinate.
It looks like a blood river.
It smells like mouldy dragon scales.
It feels like a rage of temper bursting in my brain.
It tastes like rotten nails.
It reminds me of when people wind me up.

Morgan Hopkins (8)
Our Lady & St Michael's RC Primary School, Abergavenny

Anger

Anger is red, like a burning sun with sparks flying off it.
It sounds like someone is yelling to get the ball to calm down.
It tastes like spicy hot peppers.
It smells like a puff of smoke.
It feels like a huge bag of fire in your body.
It reminds you of a dragon blowing fire.
It looks like someone pulling bulls' horns.

Anne Carrett (8)
Our Lady & St Michael's RC Primary School, Abergavenny

Love

Love is blue like birds in the sky.
It sounds like a flying mouse.
It tastes like a freshly baked muffin.
It smells like some fish and chips.
It looks like a beautiful bird in the sky.
It feels like my first day at home.
It reminds me of my Pokémon.

Daniel Taylor (8)
Our Lady & St Michael's RC Primary School, Abergavenny

Anger

Anger is as red as a bit of red rose.
It sounds like a bit of toast popping up.
It tastes like rotten toast.
It feels like a very deep feeling.
It looks like love breaking.
It smells like a bit of cheese on toast.
It's been here for thousands of years.
It reminds me of a bit of cheese caught under the fridge.

Olivia Griffiths (8)
Our Lady & St Michael's RC Primary School, Abergavenny

Happiness

Happiness is green, like a great field of flowers.
It looks like an angel from Heaven.
It smells like the best flower garden ever.
It tastes too sweet to be true.
It sounds like a choir of good spirits.
It feels like never-ending luck.
It reminds me of making new friends.

Maria James (8)
Our Lady & St Michael's RC Primary School, Abergavenny

A Wizard Is . . .

Enchanting with loads of powers,
Magical and humble, like God,
Mischievous, like an invisible shadow,
Eerie, like a haunted house,
Like a detective who has just solved a mystery.

Catriona Baker (8)
Our Lady & St Michael's RC Primary School, Abergavenny

Excited

Excited is blue like blueberries.
It looks like a juicy apple pie.
It feels like an amazing piece of ice cream.
It smells like a breeze of flowing wind.
It tastes like a beautiful smelling burger.
It sounds like a fish swimming in cold water.
It reminds me of my cruise.

Jack Meredith (8)
Our Lady & St Michael's RC Primary School, Abergavenny

Fear

Fear is like a black bat in the sky.
It sounds like a mouse running away.
It smells like people talking to you in your mind.
It tastes like a burnt chocolate cake.
It looks like you are on your own.
It reminds me of my dad.
It feels like you do not belong in the world.

Alisha Skinner (9)
Our Lady & St Michael's RC Primary School, Abergavenny

A Wizard Is . . .

Cloaked in mystery,
A mythical man and powerful
Someone who is scary and mysterious
He teaches an apprentice in sorcery
He is an intelligent man and potion master.

Matthew Gilbertson (8)
Our Lady & St Michael's RC Primary School, Abergavenny

Love

Love is pink, like a pink teddy on Valentine's Day.
It smells like a sweet, sweet cake just come out of an oven.
It feels like a gush of wind that smells like roses.
It looks like a beautiful dress just been made.
It sounds like a nice bit of chocolate being broken.
It tastes like marshmallows being cooked on a fire.
It reminds me of my pink teddy.
It does remind me of something else too . . .

Maddie Davies (8)
Our Lady & St Michael's RC Primary School, Abergavenny

A Wizard Is . . .

Like a fire and his shadow was burned,
He's gigantic but charming and enchanting,
He's hot-tempered and he burns like fire,
He is a brilliant magician,
He's talented and very interesting,
He destroys everything, even if it's a dangerous thing to do.

Mariah Reyes (8)
Our Lady & St Michael's RC Primary School, Abergavenny

A Wizard Is . . .

Spooky, he can be anything to you,
Strange, like a talking, frozen statue,
Great, like a wonderful knight,
Wonderful, like a powerful dragon,
Evil with his power.

Lucy Marsden (8)
Our Lady & St Michael's RC Primary School, Abergavenny

A Wizard Is . . .

A mysterious thing and he is very creepy.
They are also usually magical.
He is fantastically clever
Because he can remember lots of wicked spells.
He can turn you into a statue
He is so crazy that he can destroy anything in his way.
He is so lively
And he can destroy the ruler of the world.

Caszandra Erni (8)
Our Lady & St Michael's RC Primary School, Abergavenny

Love Is . . .

It looks like a little glowing light in front of you,
It tastes like a cake just out of the oven, freshly made,
It feels like a soft teddy,
It sounds like a horse,
It reminds me of being happy.

Kieran Warburton (8)
Our Lady & St Michael's RC Primary School, Abergavenny

The Shelter

I am stuck in the shelter again!
It's like a shocking pain.
Sister is shaking with fear!
I'm hugging my teddy . . .
I shiver!
    Bang! Bang!
People are crying,
Mostly suffering through dying.
I don't want this war!

Paige Newton
St Margaret's CE Primary School, Crawley

In The Air Raid Shelter

In the air raid shelter,
I am far away from home.
It is really foul
And now I need a bath.

In the air raid shelter,
It's way below a dream.
It keeps getting worse and worse,
Until it's a dreaded nightmare.

In the air raid shelter,
I'm half scared to death.
I'm really worried about my dad
And of course my mum.

When will this war go
So life,
Can become
Normal again?

Oliver Murphy
St Margaret's CE Primary School, Crawley

I'm Not Giving Up

Men are dying,
I am surviving,
I feel like declining,
But I'm not giving up.

Fear in people's eyes,
Startled, not surprised,
Children are petrified,
But I'm not giving up.

Blast! Glass shattering,
Splintering soldiers like daggers,
But I'm not giving up.

Mia Bromige
St Margaret's CE Primary School, Crawley

The Air Raid Shelter

I'm in the air raid shelter,
For the first time,
I'm jumping out my socks,
And I'm just about to cry.

I'm out of the shelter now,
So I've got my Mickey Mouse and it's foul.
I acted like my dad
And I took a great big bow.

I'm in the shelter again, *boom!*
Woah, a bomb just went off!
I'm holding onto my teddy tight,
And teddy is oh so soft.

This shelter's like a sewer,
And there are tons and tons of rats.
I'd rather fight a gorilla in pitch-black
And I'd rather see bats than these ugly rats.

Jack Donnelly (9)
St Margaret's CE Primary School, Crawley

Evacuees Whistle

The train whistle blows,
Shaken by the bombs as they whizz past.
My heart is broken.

Daddy's gone away,
Mummy's far away.
All alone!

The planes are big birds swooping by.
Mummy's crying,
I'm frying . . .

Shelby Beeden
St Margaret's CE Primary School, Crawley

The Day The Siren Was Heard

One dark, starlit night,
Searchlights are shining bright,
Bomb falls, bomb drops,
On an innocent town,
The day the siren is heard.

Quick, quick, quick,
Run, run, run,
Down the shelter,
Down you go,
Raging fires down below,
No one knows
When it will *stop*,
The day the siren is heard.

Feel the dark, damp, dingy walls,
Drip, drip,
Slip, slip,
The day the siren is heard.

Lauren Thynne (9)
St Margaret's CE Primary School, Crawley

Screams!

The night was cool and moonlit,
Wailing siren heard across whole of Devon,
Suddenly, *boom! Crash! Bang!*
Screams heard from citizens, *argh!*
They all streamed down to deep, dark shelter,
Beaming light tried piercing the moonlit cloud,
The Spitfire flew down,
Shooting its lethal weapon.
People cried for help,
Brushing against damp walls,
Smell of smoke choking people.
The all-clear siren!

Andrew Hall (9)
St Margaret's CE Primary School, Crawley

London's Nightmare

All is quiet,
All is smooth,
Until the siren wails,
Loud but slow the wail goes on,
While Bro and I race down to the backyard,
Where our strong Anderson shelter stands.
Bang! Crash! Wallop!
Dark, gloomy, scary, smelly,
Spiders on walls,
Ants on the ground,
Bang! Crash! Wallop!
Bombs dropping,
Dogs barking,
Fires crackling,
Too hot,
Too loud,
Too squashed,
It's a nightmare.
I want to get out of here!

Georgina Martin (10)
St Margaret's CE Primary School, Crawley

The Wacky War

I'm alone
I wish I was home.
People dying
I'm crying.
I'm so petrified
People are electrified.
This is a scene
I'm gonna scream.
There's an alarm
Oops, I hurt my arm.
The wacky war's over!

Shannon Bishop
St Margaret's CE Primary School, Crawley

World War Two Starts Now

Alarm rings
Choking masks on
Screams as the
Explosion thunders
Uncomfortable shelter
Shaking
Bombs smashing
Destroying homes
Afraid of the dark
Only my teddy
He was lost
I panicked
Where are my mother and father?

Robyn Edwards
St Margaret's CE Primary School, Crawley

Street Shelter

Air raid siren goes off,
Everywhere people running!
It's chaos!
I get into the street shelter,
So frightening.
Crashing,
Clanging,
It's like a raging fire speeding around.
Collapsing roofs,
Falling down,
My first time,
So puzzled.

Lewis Jones (9)
St Margaret's CE Primary School, Crawley

The War

The war began
I was sent to the country
I never wanted to go
As soon as I got there I was desperate to go back
But it was for my own good!

I missed my mum
But I couldn't go back
This was a war I couldn't understand
I was nothing without my mum
Beyond me I could see darkness
My heart was full of terror
This felt like a tremendous war!

Keanu Kellett (10)
St Margaret's CE Primary School, Crawley

Sheltered

Here I am again
In the shelter
My mum's here
So's my dad
My little sister is crying
It's our second time in here

I'm frightened
Wait . . . what's that?
Oh no! Our house has been bombed
Wait! Oh no! there's silence
Arghhh!

Aimée Wheeler
St Margaret's CE Primary School, Crawley

The Germans Are Coming!

All was still and moonlit,
Peace ruled in the town,
Then the wailing siren's shrill was heard,
A most disturbing sound.

Babies crying,
People flying,
Down to the dingy shelter they streamed,
While overhead the searchlights gazed
And put the Germans on the scene.

The shelter was cold and slimy,
Not very nice to sleep in,
While parents were worrying and nothing more
That their children they would be keeping.

Bombs crashing,
Bullets flashing,
Flying faster than light,
Then . . . *crash! Boom!*
Silence fell into the dark blue night.

Curled up in the smelly shelter,
We waited anxiously,
There it was! The all-clear wail,
To say the treacherous enemy was in the endless sea.

Heidi Mousdell (9)
St Margaret's CE Primary School, Crawley

The Raiding Horror

A clear, cold, moonlit night,
Peace is cracked, bright light shows.
With sounds so bad and siren wails,
You run to a shelter or never return.
The shelter cold, damp and dark,
Just so safe, frightening it is though.
The sounds tell you of horror,
Of terrifying fights coming.
Explosions dropping,
Crash! Smash! Bash!
An unsafe town may never return.
Shelter rattles,
Babies crying,
Dogs are barking.
Pull on your gas mask,
Quick! Quick! Quick!
Go! Go! Go!
Waiting now,
For an all-clear,
A wonderful sound,
We could stay here,
Waiting underground.
As the all-clear sounds,
An echo of relief is heard,
But who has won?
The battle of terror, horror, sadness,
And our houses in one piece!

Kathryn Doggett (9)
St Margaret's CE Primary School, Crawley

The Night I Went To The Shelter

One dark night I hear the wailing siren,
Down to the shelter I rush.

All that I can see is the searchlights
Beaming through the sky.

Crash!
I smell the flames and I have smoke in my mouth.

I can hear a baby crying,
Like a bomb coming from the air.

At last I am in the shelter,
Squashed up in a little ball.

Bang!
I hear a bomb that has dropped from 50 miles away.

I can feel rats crawling over my feet,
Like a lot of snakes wanting to be fed.

Boom!
The enemy have just shot their guns right in our way.

Siannah Scopes (9)
St Margaret's CE Primary School, Crawley

The World War Two Shelter

I'm really, really alarmed,
I wish I could go home,
I'm in the air raid shelter
And I feel like I'm alone.

I'm out the shelter now
And I'm taking a breath of air,
I feel so human now,
Because I'm out of there.

Samantha Blakey (9)
St Margaret's CE Primary School, Crawley

Blitz!

Dark, peaceful, silent night,
Children sleeping, not a stir,
Dawn is breaking, people waking,
Boom! Crash! Bang!
Siren wails, look up to the sky,
Shouting, screaming, race against time.

Down to the shelter everyone scurries,
All in a puff, all in a hurry,
Damp, dirty, hear our cries,
'We're innocent people, innocent,
Guys leave us alone!'
Bombs keep on dropping with ghastly drones.

A fearsome firebomb sent from Hell,
Came screeching down and fell into a well!
Everyone cheered, nothing was harmed.

A humming was heard,
Planes flew in the cloudy sky,
Run away, run away,
Run for your *life!*

Daisy Haggerty (10)
St Margaret's CE Primary School, Crawley

An Evacuee

I'm an evacuee
I really miss my parents
I think I'm homesick
I'm writing a letter to my mum
She said my dad has gone to war
But she said she hasn't heard from him
And that is very sad
Mum said the dog's OK
And I'm very pleased about that!

Aaliyah Kuyateh
St Margaret's CE Primary School, Crawley

My Mummy Said There's A War

My mummy said there's a war
Nothing going on
The war may be phoney
Or my mummy doesn't want me.

My mummy said there's a war
No planes, no bombs
The war may be phoney
Or Mummy doesn't want me.

My mummy said there's a war
Could it be true?
The war may be phoney
Oh no, the war is true!

Kate Turner
St Margaret's CE Primary School, Crawley

In The Air Raid Shelter

People are dying
I'm gonna start crying
I'm scared to death
But where is Beth?

I'm missing my mum
I can't find my dad!
Bombs are screaming through the sky
I'm almost going to cry!

Where am I?
I'm not very shy
I'm terrified
I really do mind!

Zoe Young (10)
St Margaret's CE Primary School, Crawley

In The Trenches

Noses are red
I feel blue
There are lice in my cabin
And I miss you.

I'm hungry, I'm thirsty
There's noise all around
Germans approaching
Our English ground.

Doom is waiting round the bend
For each and every man
I wonder when the war will end
I'll survive it if I can.

Georgina Reeves (9)
St Margaret's CE Primary School, Crawley

The Shelter

Away from home
In a smelly street shelter
Then the rattle grates
Gas masks on!

The shells are whirling
Winds howling
My senses are frayed
Mind confused and scared.

An hour has passed
Shell-shocked faces
Baby screaming -

This is World War II.

Georgia Harman (10)
St Margaret's CE Primary School, Crawley

The Deadly Air Raid

On a moonlit night,
The stars were shining bright,
I heard the deadly siren,
Then I ran down the street,
With the sound of rain dripping on my feet.

A lady started shouting,
I ran towards the noise,
My stomach started churning,
As I ran to a house with a shelter,
I heard a *crash* of a bomb.

When I was there
I had run out of puff,
But I ran into the shelter,
And closed the door with a bang!

I started to slow my breathing,
But then I heard another bang,
My breathing got faster,
Then I jumped into a bed,
The bed was not comfy,
But it would do for now.

The lights flickered
As I was hiding in the bed,
I could feel drips coming off the ceiling,
Then I put my gas mask on,
Suddenly, the light dimmed then it went out,
I was left alone in the darkness,
All alone and no one to talk to.

My stomach churned
As I worried about getting hurt,
I started sobbing as the ceiling started to fall,
I screamed with fright
As a bomb fell in the shelter,
My life ruined by a bomb.

Ella Pickford (9)
St Margaret's CE Primary School, Crawley

The Night The Siren Was Heard

Star bright, moon light,
A peaceful night in London,
Then a horrid sound was heard,
The wailing sirens, Germans!

It was a race for life,
To the damp, dark shelter,
Stumbling, staggering people,
Down the hill they flew.

Hurried along the road,
To find a safe shelter,
They didn't even care
If it had rats!

Some ran in their gardens,
Some rushed to the tube station,
Some crawled into a Morrison shelter,
To save their sorry lives.

I could hear rustling rats,
I could feel squashed people,
I could smell all sorts of things,
The night I went to the shelter.

I felt scared,
I was hungry,
I was thirsty,
I didn't know what to do.

Ashleigh Hill (9)
St Margaret's CE Primary School, Crawley

A Night To Remember

The moon hung low,
The stars were high,
As passing planes flew by.
Searchlights beamed,
To spot the enemy,
The siren's wail was heard,
A night to remember.

Innocent people flooded London,
People's screams destroyed all happiness.
Citizens streamed into the shelter,
While fighters appeared around every corner.
The bombs scared people for life,
But still the guns rang out,
A night to remember.

Down in the shelter,
Benches as hard as rock.
The buzz of chatter could be heard,
But all I could think of was
Would my house be standing?
A night to remember.

Beth Murphy (9)
St Margaret's CE Primary School, Crawley

War Began

Midnight strikes, church clock sounds,
Spotlights beaming in the sky,
Spotting Germans.

British fighters saving our country,
Guns firing, smoke gathering,
People dying, children crying.

People rushing into shelters,
Scrambling, pulling,
Trying to survive the horrible war.

Sam Aston (9)
St Margaret's CE Primary School, Crawley

Air Raid Emergency!

The night was dark and spooky,
The wailing siren was heard,
People from all over streamed across the countryside,
The blasting bombs were dropping,
All citizens hurried underground,
It was a race against time.

'Down to the shelter everyone!' the warden demanded.
Everyone hurried down,
All in a puff,
The booming bombs were dropping,
All you could hear was a monstrous *boom* and *crash!*
Shivers ran down the terrified citizens' spines.

Bombs were as loud as an asteroid crashing to the ground,
Children cuddled parents,
Walls dripping with water,
Rats scurried over feet,
People squashed and crammed,
Wondering if their houses were still standing,
Lethal Spitfire shot down deadly bombers,
All kinds of planes flew through the moonlit sky,
'Don't worry everyone, we'll be OK!' shouts the warden.

Sarah Soloman (10)
St Margaret's CE Primary School, Crawley

The Shelter

I've gone to the shelter
Sister's crying
Bombs are flying past me like a train
What's it like out there?
Probably a nightmare
I'm having bad dreams
I ask my mummy
'When is the war over?'

Zachary Lampey (9)
St Margaret's CE Primary School, Crawley

In A Fighter Plane

Yet again in this cramped fighter plane
Thousands of shells
I want home
Horrid swooping, soaring
Dodging, diving
Fighting for London
Fighting for England
It might be the end
It might be the beginning!

Samuel Lashwood
St Margaret's CE Primary School, Crawley

The Final Hour

I'm on the front line
People are crying
Others are declining in front of me
Ow! I've been splattered in blood
Others are hiding in mud
Bombs are dropping
I'm in a bit of a palaver
I'm stuck in my armour!

Christian Clark (9)
St Margaret's CE Primary School, Crawley

Air Raid

Night was dark, frosty and cold
Air raid siren wailing on and off
Citizens flooding the streets of London
To get to a shelter
Doodlebugs flying overhead.

People dying, lights shaking
Babies crying
Aeroplanes dropping.

Matthew Clipperton (9)
St Margaret's CE Primary School, Crawley

The Owl

The yellow moon floating across the blue night sky,
While she turns her head and looks for food.
Tu-whit, tu-whoo, tu-whit, tu-whoo, tu-whit, tu-whoo,
The owl has seen food.
As she glides across the night sky,
She feels very happy.

Alfie Woodrow (8)
St Mary's Primary School, Roughton

The Bluebird

I see a bluebird,
Collecting twigs for its nest,
Flying tree to tree,
Bright bluebird flying
Like a speeding dart.
Chubby little bluebird,
Dodging the cats,
Silky, smooth feathers,
Getting worms,
Making a cheeping noise.

Chloe Mason (8)
St Mary's Primary School, Roughton

The Bat

Glides across the summer moon,
It does not make a sound,
In the day it sleeps,
It flies in the night,
It's as sly as a fox,
As it swoops it eats flies.

Phoebe Chambers (8)
St Mary's Primary School, Roughton

Ten Things In A Knight's Bag

A rusty crash helmet,
A wooden sword,
Armour made out of glass,
Spurs made out of plugs,
A horse that has tiger skin,
A belt made of cardboard,
A saddle made of metal,
A lance made out of glass,
An oil can with no oil in it!
Boots made of plastic!
Knight's list to catch a dragon:
I will need:
Cage, bazooka, rope and grenade.

Matthew Andrews (8)
St Mary's Primary School, Roughton

My Cat

My cat lives in a castle
My cat can skip with a rope
My cat can ride a quad bike
My cat is my best friend
My cat can go on the trampoline
My cat can hop along a wall
My cat is not like other cats
My cat can't miaow at all!

Rhiannon Stanton (8)
St Mary's Primary School, Roughton

Ten Things Found In A Knight's Pocket

A rusty crash helmet
A wooden sword
Armour made of shoe boxes
An old belt made of shiny pink paper
A horse wearing pyjamas
Spurs made of ice
A plastic saddle
An ugly princess
A servant who is always asleep
And a map with only one half!

Tequila Sayer (9)
St Mary's Primary School, Roughton

List Poem

My carp loves going to Butlins
My carp's best friend is a roach
My carp weighs thirty-five pounds
My carp can climb a tree
My carp loves eating marshmallows
My carp enjoys playing baseball
My carp is not like other fish
My carp can't flap its fins at all.

Jordon Storey (9)
St Mary's Primary School, Roughton

Ten Things In A Knight's Bag

A rusty crash helmet,
A wooden sword,
Armour made out of plastic,
An old belt made of wrapping paper,
A dead horse,
Spurs that jingle and rattle,
A sharp saddle,
A pair of rusty old boots,
A rag princess
And a paper shield!

Bethany Griffin (8)
St Mary's Primary School, Roughton

My Cat

Slumping on a soft, fluffy pillow like a cloud,
Moving quietly to pounce on a mouse,
A black and white cat like a sleek broom,
A body like a large balloon,
Fur as smooth as silk,
Purrs like a tractor's engine.
My cat's *purrfect!*

Chloe Lewis (8)
St Mary's Primary School, Roughton

Best Friends

B est friends are not like
E ach other. We always
S tand with each other on
T hursdays and every other day.

F riends are the best, not like the
R est. They are always there
I n school or out.
E ven when I am down
N ever leave me out
D oing all that fun stuff at
S chool or at my house.

Sophie Titlow (10)
Saxlingham Nethergate Primary School, Norwich

The Garden Poem

Leaves, leaves falling off the trees
Wherever you walk you're treading on leaves.
I keep on trying to rake them up
But I have no luck.
They just keep getting everywhere
Grass, grass everywhere, you're treading on grass
Wherever you go it needs a cut.
It's growing and growing because of the rain
It rains nearly every day, but more like every week.

Eliza Bolton (8)
Saxlingham Nethergate Primary School, Norwich

A Winter Wonderland

A frosted window sits in front of me
As I stare out into the winter wonderland,
I see a white, fluffy blanket of snow
Lying on the frozen ground,
An icy breeze moves by the door
And into the room,
I stare out of the frosted window once more,
I see shimmering, piercing icicles
Sparkling like diamonds as the sun warms the skies
To end the winter,
The snowman really takes the hint
Of the wintry world outdoors,
I looked out of the frosted window
And that's what I saw.

Alana Emms (9)
Saxlingham Nethergate Primary School, Norwich

Teddies

I love teddies
I really, really do
I love teddies
How about you?

Teddies are fluffy, lovely and cuddly
Teddies help you get to sleep
Teddies are soft, loveable and huggable
Teddies tell you secrets
My teddy is fluffy, lovely, cuddly, soft
Loveable and huggable
My teddy helps me get to sleep
And tells me secrets
My teddy is *Teddy!*

Sammy O'Connor Balsillie (10)
Saxlingham Nethergate Primary School, Norwich

Edward VI

He was king at the age of 9 in Tudor times
But he died aged 18 chimes.
He had a pet hawk but he tore out its feathers
The poor bird caught methers

His siblings were two sisters
But he had no brothers
A germ sneaked into Edward's bed
It killed him dead

His mother died at his birth
And his father died of old age turph
Poor Edward had a very short life
Nor had time to find a wife

His eldest sister, Mary, became Queen
But she was very mean
She was known as 'Bloody Mary' for her cruelty
But what she didn't know was she was her doomery.

Cameron Cawley (8)
Saxlingham Nethergate Primary School, Norwich

Guinea Piglets

You are . . .
As squeaky as a mouse
And you nibble your grass house.
You are furry
You are very sniffy and kissy.
You are as cheeky as a monkey
As bouncy as a baby bunny.
Naughty and funny
My two baby guinea girls.

Eleanor Beadle (8)
Sele First School, Hexham

Oi, Ref!

Oi, ref!
Penalty!
We should have had
Twenty!

Oi, ref!
It crossed the line
We think you've
Been drinking wine!

Oi, ref!
That was a goal!
And you said
It hit the pole!

Oi, ref!
The throw-in's ours!
Do you think
You've got magical powers?

Oi, ref!
Yellow card!
He kicked our player
And he missed the shin guard!

Oi, ref!
Send him off!
Now he's punched our player,
Biff, boff, boff!

Oi, ref,
Good match, good game!
3-1 to us,
Will you ref for us again?

Matthew Hutton (8)
Sele First School, Hexham

Alfie Moon

I have a little pony
His name is Alfie Moon
He always hears me coming
When I sing my merry tune.

I greet him with a loving pat
Upon his velvety nose
But all he seems to want
Is his bucket full of oats.

Alfie loves to gallop around
Over fields and maisy meadows
Alfie likes to jump and play
All through the day.

When we come home
All tired and happy
He loves a juicy carrot
Yum, yum, yummy!

In his stable all warm and cosy
He snuggles into his straw and goes all dozy
I love my little pony
He is my bestest friend.

I'll love my little Alfie
I'll love him till the end.

Matthew Stokes (8)
Sele First School, Hexham

Happy Day With Best Friend

Oh my, oh my, oh my
What will I do today
Not a cloud in the sky
I think I will go out and play

Running around in the garden
It really is such fun
Here's my best friend, Martin
With his shoelaces undone

'Boys, it's time for lunch'
I heard my mummy cry
Fish and chips would be my hunch
But no, it is shepherd's pie

'Now it's time for me to go home'
Martin said with a sigh
My mummy's just been on the phone
So I really must say bye-bye.

Ben Shotton (8)
Sele First School, Hexham

I Love My Life

I read a story today
That touched me deep inside,
It made me realise
I'm happy to be alive.

I read a story today
About a boy who drowned,
It must have been very sad
When he was found.

I read a story today
I'm glad that I'm alive,
I care about my family
And everything around.

I love my life!

Oliver Slipman (8)
Sele First School, Hexham

The Long Walk

I wanted to go on a big long walk
My granda thought I was all talk
I wanted to carry on over the hill
But there wasn't time
    It's getting dark
    It's going to rain
    You'll never make it
Then on Saturday it just fitted the bill
Sun shining, pack on back, off we strode
To the sign on the gate, mile and a half to the Military Road
We lost the path, so stopped for a bit
Then continued on looking for the next gate
There was a hare, two deer and plenty of birds
But not another person stirred
Then there it was, in the distance
The Roman temple to the God Mithos
I'd made it, I'd made it, thank goodness for that
We stopped and ate again from the pack
All I had to do was make it back.

Kieran Stewart (9)
Sele First School, Hexham

My Cat, Martha

Martha is my favourite cat,
Even though she is so fat.
She sleeps all day at the bottom of the bed,
With her paw across her head.
When she wakes up she looks for food,
To put her in a very good mood.
She scratches Dad, she scratches me,
The one she loves is my mummy.
Martha is a lovely mog,
But I really would prefer a dog.

Oscar Goncalves (8)
Sele First School, Hexham

The Best Thing Is Art

Art is messy
Art is funny
Sometimes my pictures get all runny
Paintbrushes are fat
Paintbrushes are thin
But my paintbrush is as thin as a pin
Some paints are bright
Some paints are dark
I even have paints that glow in the dark
I've got glitter on the ceiling
I've got glitter on the floor
I don't know how, but there's glitter on the door
Paper is white
Paper is coloured
But my paper is multicoloured
Art is the best
Art is my thing
I love art so much
That it makes my head spin.

Alice Merriman-Jones (8)
Sele First School, Hexham

My Cat, Sox

M oves like a crazed creature
Y ellow eyes stare powerfully at you

C limbs walls like Spider-Man
A ttacks flies . . . and spiders!
T ickling her tummy's her favourite

S ox is her name, Pantz is her sister
O n my bed she curls up
X rays at the vets she hates!

Heather Battye (8)
Sele First School, Hexham

Recycle

Recycle your rubbish
Turn off the lights
Save your energy
And things will be alright

Crush your tins
And crush your cans
Walk to school
Don't use vans

If you use paper
Use both sides
Remember global warming
It changes the tides

Make your own compost
Throw things in the waste
Put it on the garden
It will give it a better taste.

Kerri Tron (8)
Sele First School, Hexham

The Haunted House

It creaked like chalk on a blackboard,
As I slowly opened the door,
My hand shook as I held the doorknob,
I couldn't take it anymore,
My foot slowly moved forward,
Closer to the thing with the claw.

Fear is the only thing to describe it,
In a blink it was all over,
As the claw painfully sliced my chest,
As everything got darker,
Now I am the ghost of this house!

Harrison Mann (8)
Sele First School, Hexham

My Favourite Book

My favourite book is 'Cat In The Hat' today,
It's about a boy and a girl who were left home to play.
The cat came in and messed up the house,
Funny enough, there wasn't even a mouse.
The kids got worried when the house was a tip,
The Cat in the Hat made a quick trip.
He brought back a red box with thing 1 and thing 2
And told them to clean the house, but they didn't do.
The boy and girl had to make them stop,
So they threw the net over their heads with a plop!
They managed to clean the house very fast,
So the Cat in the Hat left the house at last.
Their mother came home early in the day,
So the kids had more time to have fun and to play.

Stella Anastasiou (8)
Sele First School, Hexham

My Kitten

I brought my kittens home
They'd left their mum
They felt alone.
They shook and trembled
Like an autumn leaf
Their lonely faces full of grief.

Not long until they'd settled in
Our house has no place left unexplored
The curtains show the marks of their teeny, furry claws.
They are in and out of the cupboards
Up and down the stairs
Like tiny, teeny whirlwinds, they rush everywhere.

Louis Edwards (8)
Sele First School, Hexham

All Year Round

Spring is a time when all the flowers grow
All of the trees start to blossom
Fresh colours on all of the flowers everywhere you look
Then Easter comes, there are bonnet parades and lots of eggs.

Summer comes after and it's time for your holidays
Barbecues are popular with burgers and sausages
Playing outside and having ice creams is fun
You go to the countryside and have a picnic.

Autumn is here and all the golden leaves are falling off the trees
Fireworks come and *bang, bang, bang!*
The weather is getting chillier
Hallowe'en happens and costumes are brought out.

Winter arrives with all its frost and ice
Christmas is here with presents and trees
The nights get darker and soon it's pitch-black
It's time for snowball fights and making snowmen and snow angels.

Hamish Forsyth (8)
Sele First School, Hexham

Football Crazy

The match kicked off on grass of green
The men in blue were on the scene
On the other team the men in red
They looked like they were still in bed
Ronaldo kicked the ball with might
The crowd above screamed, 'What a sight!'
The ball swished straight into the net
It simply cannot be over yet
The match ended one-nil down
The losing team put on a frown
And vowed to beat them next time round.

James Carruthers (8)
Sele First School, Hexham

At The Seaside

Bucket and spade in my hand,
Moving swiftly across the sand,
Having fun all day long,
Building sandcastles for the sea to destroy,
Going fishing in the boat and
Maybe see a basking shark,
Going shrimping in the pool,
Maybe catch a crab or two,
When the sun shines above you,
It's so nice to be at the beach,
In the sea diving down,
Doing handstands, splashing around,
Then the sun goes away,
Say goodbye and run to bed.

Chloe Davey (8)
Sele First School, Hexham

Opposites

Big to small, low to tall,
Different things from new to old,
Writing from thin to bold,
Elephant and mouse, igloo to house,
Thick and thin, bottom to brim,
Land and water, son and daughter,
Good and bad, happy and sad,
Smile and frown, up and down,
Girl and boy, gloom and joy,
Minus and add, mum and dad,
Black and white, day and night,
Love and hate, marry and date,
Sun and moon, morning and noon,
CD or tape, early and late.

Megan Ashford (8)
Sele First School, Hexham

Winter's Coming

Winter's coming,
Mornings chilly.
Winter's coming,
I'm looking silly,
(Wrapped up in hat,
gloves and scarf!)
Hurry up, it's school today,
Don't forget a coat
When you go to play.
Playing outside
In the cold fresh air,
Beginning to wish
The weather was fair.
Winter's coming,
Wrap up warm,
Winter's coming,
Watch out for the storm.

Abigail Thomson (8)
Sele First School, Hexham

My Birthday

It's my birthday soon,
We will have a party at noon.
My friends will come and play,
It will be a very special day.
We will have sandwiches and cake
And enough juice to fill a lake.
The pressies I get stand taller than me
And if I get any more,
They will be as big as a tree.
At the end of the day,
My friends come and say,
Thanks Daniel,
That was a great birthday.

Daniel Hope (8)
Sele First School, Hexham

The Year

January brings the frost and snow
And all the while the cold winds blow.
February doesn't get any better,
Now it's sleet and rain, much, much better.
March kicks in with very little change,
But bounces out with hares acting strange.
April gets warmer, flower beds start to fill,
A lonely poet would write about a daffodil.
May gets hot and summer is on the way,
Strange men called Morris have their day.
June gets hotter days after the nights get lighter in every way.
July stays the same,
Sitting in the garden playing games.
August sees me on the beach being cool,
Life can't be better because I'm not at school.
September has got bad bits I know, but then
Next year doesn't matter because I'll be ten.
October is a bit colder, but that's the case,
Indian summers happen but it's still happy days.
November, November, there's something to remember,
Guy Fawkes gets charred and burnt to an ember.
December's freezing, but it's not something I resent,
As long as my mum and dad give me a great big present.

Luke James McCormick (9)
Sele First School, Hexham

The Nonsense Poem

The sea and a great ocean got in a commotion
And made the pretty, purple-scaled mermaids sing to the
                              sky-blue dolphins.
But suddenly, the sky went grey for a thunderstorm,
As Portugal flew under the waves of tumbling pearls.

Dorothy Hakim (8)
Sele First School, Hexham

Changing Seasons

Spring is when it gets warmer,
Spring is when the green leaves grow back on the trees,
Spring is when the beautiful flowers start to grow,
Spring is when the hedgehogs come out of hibernation
And the birds start to sing.

Summer is when the days get longer and hotter,
Summer is when the sky is blue and the grass is green,
Summer is when the gardens bloom with flowers,
Summer is when we can go to the beach and build sandcastles.

Autumn is when it starts to get colder,
Autumn is when the leaves dry up and fall off the trees,
Autumn is when the trees are bare,
Autumn is when the beautiful summer flowers die.

Winter is when it gets really cold,
Winter is when the days get shorter and darker,
Winter is when Jack Frost makes it frosty in the mornings,
Winter is when it starts to snow and our sledges can come out.

Tony Crozier (8)
Sele First School, Hexham

My Pet Rabbits

I have two little rabbits
They are very special to me
They are Dutch and live in a hutch
As cosy as can be.

Their coats are black and white
Which show up well in the night
They dig big holes but *not* like moles
And munch carrots for their tea.

Hannah Pinkney (8)
Sele First School, Hexham

The Seaside

S oft, sandy beaches filled with laughing children running in the sea,
    as playful as puppies
E ndless sparkling sea, glinting in the morning sunlight
A blazing sun, shining over the glistening sea
S ounds of plastic spades being dug into the soft sand
I ce creams melting on a smooth, shiny rock
D aring rock climbers buckling their tight harnesses and tugging
    strong ropes
E verybody screaming and running about, jumping over
    enormous waves.

Rachel Wood (8)
Sele First School, Hexham

Football Team

F antastic fans cheering from the terraces
O n the pitch came the eager footballers
O nly the opposition to overcome
T he referee blows the whistle and they're
B ooting the ball up and down the pitch
A ttacking play with the ball at your feet
L ooking for space to pass the ball
L obbing the ball over the keeper's head

T ackling the ball from the midfielders
E njoying the match as the fans cheer
A ccurate shooting in front of goal
M atch ends 3-1 to our team, hip, hip, *hooray!*

Luke Allman (8)
Sele First School, Hexham

The Sunshine State

Florida is the best
The turquoise skies and beaches
Better than the rest

I can see the horizon of the sea
Crashing and smashing
Like nothing you could ever see

Swimming pools, warm and inviting
Jumping, splashing
How exciting

I went to Magic Kingdom
I was scared and wet
Then I went on Space Mountain
I was as scared as I could get.

Erin Rodgers (8)
Sele First School, Hexham

The Big Game

F amily fun
O h, what a game
O ohs and aahs
T ackling and tugging to get the ball
B oos and shouts of 'bravo' from the crowd
A ttacking your opponent to get the ball
L ook how well the team is playing
L eft foot scores a goal. *Yay!*

Jake McPherson (8)
Sele First School, Hexham

Match Madness

Frantic footie fans cheer loudly at
The players on the pitch.
The waving black and white scarves.

Ref covered in black
Shows yellow card, blows the whistle, *peep!*

Bouncing, round ball,
Dribble and weave, past the defence.
Pass! Shoot! Score! Goal! Hooray!

Colourful, stripy strips,
Run across the pitch.
Mark him! Penalty! Offside!
Glorious, golden goals.

Seats towering above,
Stadium closing over our heads.
Players hug each other and
Shake hands with the other team.

Sam Ridealgh (8)
Sele First School, Hexham

Football

F ootball is fun, it's the best game ever
O utside in the sunny weather
O verjoyed when you score a goal
T he corner kick is taken by a pole
B right blue shirts and yellow around
A mazing noises come from inside the ground
L osing is the worst feeling ever, but always pull yourself together
L ifting the terrific trophy high, we've broken the records *forever!*

Calum Thomas (9)
Sele First School, Hexham

Seasons

In summer the sun is hot
In summer the horses go *trot*
In summer you get refreshing ice cream
In summer the stars beam
I love summer

In autumn the leaves are falling
In autumn the wind is calling
In autumn the sun is gentle
I love autumn

In winter the sun is low
In winter there is a Christmas show
In winter I am cold
I love winter

But best of all
In spring the birds are tweeting
In spring me and my friends are meeting
I love spring.

Annie McCormick (8)
Sele First School, Hexham

Frosty Night

My toasty toes tucked in tight
To boots that crunch and scrunch the ice.
Stars sparkle ever so bright
On this beautiful, crisp, wintry night.
The moon glimmers, shedding warmth and light,
Leading me home to my bed where I snuggle so tight.

Holly Griffiths (8)
Sele First School, Hexham

Christmas

Not long now, I need to write my list
I've been good, but has my sis?
I hang my calendar on the door
Tomorrow I open 24.
I hear the sleigh bells in my sleep
I must remember not to peep!
I walk downstairs in the morning
Mummy and Daddy are still snoring.
I see my presents on the chair
My heart's beating fast, I can only stare.
As I eat my Christmas lunch
Around the table are a chattering bunch.
Time for bed, I brush my hair
Christmas is over for another year.

Catherine Brotherton (8)
Sele First School, Hexham

Music

Music running through my ears
Music so loud I cannot hear
Guitars and drums playing together
A brilliant sound, may it last forever
I feel joyful as the music blasts
I dance wildly while it lasts
The music echoing in my brain
Softly now, the tune's on the wane
I feel sad now as it fades away
But it's always with me, not just today.

Elizabeth Dracup (9)
Sele First School, Hexham

Autumn

Autumn is here, frost in the morning,
Dew upon the grass,
Leaves fall, spiral, turn and twist from their homes,
Hues of purple, gold, brown and red all tumbling down,
I love to crunch my feet on the leaves,
All crisp and dry underfoot
And then the wind comes and whisks them away
Into a whirlwind high above my head,
Next is the rain, wet, cold and hard,
My beautiful leaves are now mush.

James Hagon (8)
Sele First School, Hexham

A Whale Of A Tale

I have a friend, she's a whale,
She has a massive, big blue tail.
She splashes and lashes,
But she's really gentle,
She never really goes crazy, mental.
Swimming gracefully,
She swims in a ladylike way,
She flows with the waves
And her name is May.
Yes, that's my friend,
The big blue whale.

Roslyn Box (8)
Sele First School, Hexham

The Meadow

A trillion trees loom behind
The windswept meadow,
And in the corner, shamed and wrecked,
Huddles a small shed.
Next to it stands a silent gate,
Weeds and grass grow in the meadow,
Sweet scented flowers shimmer
Through the woven brambles.
A cat lurks on a plain wooden post,
Staring straight at the listing gate.
This meadow is filled with happiness
As the birds charm the sky.
If you stand in the midst of it all,
You can smell the midsummer winding around you.

Neema Mwande (9)
Sele First School, Hexham

Football And Me

Football is my favourite thing,
Football is the best,
Kicking a ball is great fun
And scoring is a joy.
Winning matches is OK,
But being in a team means the most.
Training with friends matters to me,
Having fun is what it's all about.

Alistair Scott (9)
Sele First School, Hexham

My Summer Holiday

We are off on holiday in a plane,
Our suitcases are neatly packed.
The place we are visiting is the south of Spain,
In one week we will be flying back.

I love to watch the deep blue sea
And play on the golden sand,
Collect lots of beautiful shells
To feel them with my hand.

The clear, blue sea is lovely and warm,
I love to dodge the waves,
Above my head the seagulls swarm,
Then head off back to their caves.

Holly Atkinson (8)
Sele First School, Hexham

Football

Football is my favourite sport
Football every day
Football on the PlayStation
Football, hip hip hooray
It's *B*lackburn v Newcastle
And it's still 0-0
Shearer flies and does a roll
Look Newcastle have scored a goal!

Seamus Libretto (8)
Sele First School, Hexham

Christmas

C People singing *carols* in the dark streets
H The bright red berries decorating the *holly* bushes
R The jingle of *Rudolph's* bells
I I like to help my mama *icing* the crumbly Christmas cake
S The brilliant white *snow*
T The tall, proud Christmas *tree* with its twinkling lights
M I wonder how many boys I will kiss under the *mistletoe?*
A The sweet smell of chocolate from the *Advent* calendar
S The bright, shining *star* that beams out over the Christmas tree.

Kirsty Brotherton (8)
Sele First School, Hexham

Autumn

A sky of sapphire-blue
Emerald grass waving in the breeze
A sparkly stream bubbling and flowing
Birds all singing, perched on trees
Cows grazing, gently mooing
Insects humming, buzzing bees
Leaves - orange, yellow, red, slowly falling from the trees
Juicy blackberries and scarlet apples
Spiky holly and prickly thorns
Crunchy leaves and shiny conkers
A towering oak tree with many acorns.

Alexander Birkinshaw (8)
Sele First School, Hexham

Summer

Summer is wonderful,
Bright and cheerful,
The glistening sun shines over you.
The grass is fresh,
The sun is yellow
And the sky is blue.

Summer feels light,
Cheerful and bright,
I am set free!
The sand at the beach,
Feels soft on my feet,
Whoopee!

Erin Brook (8)
Sele First School, Hexham

Going On Holiday

Going on holiday
The best treat of the year
Pack the cases
Get in the car
Go to the airport
Because we're travelling far
Here we are on the plane
Going to North Africa again and again
Arrived at last
We'll have such a blast
Playing football, going to the pool
It really is very cool.

James Mitchell (8)
Sele First School, Hexham

I Could Be?

I could be a gorilla,
Mighty, strong and tough,
I could be an elephant,
With powerful, long tusks.
I could be a rhino,
Charging everywhere,
I could be a tiger,
Pouncing from my lair.
I could be a crocodile,
Lurking in the river,
I could be a lion,
Making people quiver.
I could be a cheetah,
Running for my prey,
I could be a monkey,
Curious all day.
I could be a hippo,
River horse, quite funny,
I could be a bear,
Looking for some honey.
I could be a giraffe,
Tall and proud with grace,
I could be a mouse,
In a tiny hiding place.
In fact I could be anything,
In my head's the information,
For when I fall asleep at night,
I use my *imagination*.

Cody Thompson (8)
Sele First School, Hexham

Sammy The Hammy

Sammy was cool
He was my favourite pet
He was brown and white
And came out at night

Sammy was always hungry
From out of his bedding
He would peek
And he stuffed food in his cheek

Sammy was energetic
He liked to run around
He only had a short tail
But he could run faster than a snail

Sammy was sometimes noisy
He played with his water bottle
He was a music-maker
When he rattled it like a shaker

Sammy was cool
He was my favourite pet
He was cute and cuddly
And I miss him lots.

Alex Kellas (8)
Sele First School, Hexham

Monkeys

Monkeys, monkeys are a happy bunch,
When they eat bananas their teeth go *crunch*.
Each day they swing from tree to tree
And sometimes they get stung by a bee.

Sometimes they get carried on their mother's back,
Or sometimes bounce about like a jumping jack.
They always play tricks on each other,
Even though they love each other.

When it's bedtime they cuddle together,
So they keep warm forever and ever.
My daddy says I'm his little monkey,
Even though he is a bit chunky!

Thomas Jepson (8)
Sele First School, Hexham

My Holiday In Paris

This summer we went to Paris
My mum and dad and me
We also took Miranda
She's part of our family

We flew there in an aeroplane
High up in the sky
The plane was coloured orange
To home we said goodbye

We saw the Eiffel Tower
It was very tall
For breakfast we had croissants
That was the best of all.

Olivia Fenwick (8)
Sele First School, Hexham

Chloe The Cat

Chloe is the family cat,
She likes to sleep on her fluffy mat.
She is grey and white,
Her eyes are green and bright.

She is quite old,
She sleeps and sleeps,
Even when she is out in the cold.

She loves her food
And cries for more,
Even when her tummy is full and sore.

She cuddles up
When you are sitting on the sofa,
She likes her tummy tickled all over.

Penny Parr (8)
Sele First School, Hexham

The Effort Chart

Holly has tons of ticks while Tanya has none,
Tanya's friends with Penny who has just one.

Cameron got all his ticks so he won a prize,
He chose a medal, you should have seen the size!

The boy who's done the best, he's called Bill,
The rest are in the middle, happy with their skill.

And now the year is over, a new chart's begun,
The next class has started, ready for some fun!

Zoë Hardy (8)
Sele First School, Hexham

Hallowe'en, Hallowe'en

Hallowe'en, Hallowe'en, super-scary night,
Hallowe'en, Hallowe'en, give your friends a fright!
See the sight of witches' sharp, pointy hats and
See the spooky grin of frightening pumpkins looking at you all night.
Hallowe'en, Hallowe'en, teeth chattering,
Hallowe'en, Hallowe'en, bones shattering!
Smell the smell of witches' cauldrons bubbling their potions,
Smell the smell of rotting teeth crunching and snapping at sweets!
Hallowe'en, Hallowe'en, skeletons and souls,
Hallowe'en Hallowe'en, did someone fall down a hole?
Could this be the scariest, spookiest Hallowe'en ever?
Wait, what about last year? An absolute, *never!*

Cameron Wilson (8)
Sele First School, Hexham

History! History!

History! History! What can you tell?
You're waking my brain up with a big, booming bell.
History! History! We love it all,
Makes me feel strong and tall.
History! History! Makes me cry thinking of times gone by,
How many times has there been lots that I have not seen?
Some of them that were quite mean.

Thomas Barnes (8)
Sele First School, Hexham

Seasons

All the seasons have a name:
Spring, summer, autumn, winter.
Spring is the first season,
I don't know why, I'm sure there's a reason.
Next is summertime,
With leafy trees to hide in and climb.
Third is autumn -
My cousin was running in the dead leaves, so I caught him.
Finally, it's winter though
With wind and rain and thick soft snow.
Sometimes there's a big rainbow!
So there are the seasons
And the reasons,
Now it's time for me to go.

Frannie Wise (8)
Sele First School, Hexham

Blood . . . War . . . Death!

The sound of men yelling 'charge!'
The bang of shields smacking each other
The spears penetrating through men's guts
The cracking of the men's bones
The boiling hot sun blocking the men's eyes
The shouts of men getting killed
The arrows darkening the skies
The horses' hooves thundering across the plain.

Ruby McCormick (8)
Sele First School, Hexham

Middle School

I went to my new school last night
To have a look around,
I start there in the autumn term
And hope to get about.
There's lots of classrooms there,
Science, art and English,
Geography, history and French,
ICT, music and I saw my friends as well.
My friends and I had cookies
In the school canteen,
I'm looking forward to next year
With all the things I've seen.

Hannah Harling (8)
Sele First School, Hexham

All Year Round - Haikus

Prancing leprechauns
Munching Easter bunnies' eggs
In snow rising up.

Lazy daisies rest
Sunny days are long and hot
Till misty morn comes.

In dawn's misty swirls
Conkers sleep on leafy beds
While the starbursts fall.

Snug people walk on
Slippery roads, broken cars
Happy New Year's Day.

Cameron Tibbles (8)
Sele First School, Hexham

Fluffy Bunnies

Fluffy furballs running about
Floppy ears hearing sounds
Twitchy noses smelling carrots
Silky whiskers catching the wind
Soft fur just like velvet
Pompom tails, fluffy as can be
Leaping about on the grass
That's fluffy bunnies.

Grace Percival (8)
Sele First School, Hexham

Muffin, My Hamster

H aving fun in her ball
A t night she runs around
M ornings she is fast asleep
S ometimes she bites the bars
T iny teeth nibble food
E ating everything up
R eally happy, Muffin.

Amy Donaldson
Sele First School, Hexham

At The Park

Up, down, all around
Side to side and upside down
Up above looking all around
Singing, dancing, mucking around
At the park, time to play
Yippee! It's time again.

Jake Dunlop (8)
Sele First School, Hexham

Happy

Happy is green, like trees.
It sounds like children shouting.
It tastes like olives.
It smells like flowers.
It looks like a bee.
It feels like a roller coaster.
It reminds me of my dog.

Matthew Panes (8)
Sporle CE Primary School, King's Lynn

Love

Love is red like roses.
It sounds like kisses.
It smells like chocolate.
It tastes like strawberries.
It looks like lips.
It feels like he really loves me.
It reminds me of my boyfriend.

Sarah Hunt (8)
Sporle CE Primary School, King's Lynn

Excited

Excited is gold like a block of gold.
It sounds like a bell.
It tastes like cake.
It smells like cooking food.
It looks like hope.
It feels like fun.
It reminds me of games.

Cameron Willis (8)
Sporle CE Primary School, King's Lynn

Sad

Sad is blue like the sea.
It sounds like a dropping apple.
It tastes like a spoonful of disgusting medicine.
It smells like a pile of disgusting socks.
It looks like a big list of chores.
It feels painful and unkind.
It reminds me of someone dying.

Zoë Hembling (8)
Sporle CE Primary School, King's Lynn

Excited

Excited is gold like the sun
It sounds like a bonfire
It tastes like yummy sausages
It smells like meaty meat
It looks like a nice, juicy apple
It feels like a fork
It reminds me of my first PlayStation game.

Matthew Wilkins (9)
Sporle CE Primary School, King's Lynn

Angry

Angry is a dark red like blood.
It sounds like ghosts screaming.
It smells like raw cabbage.
It looks all twisted.
It feels all spiky and prickly.
It reminds me of my brother.

Harrison Bond (8)
Sporle CE Primary School, King's Lynn

Excited

Excited is yellow, like a fruity banana,
It sounds like when Manchester United score a goal,
It tastes like a very tasty and meaty hot dog,
It smells like a freshly cooked evening meal,
It looks like a shooting star,
It feels like a squidgy rubber,
It reminds me of Christmas Day.

Charlotte Simmons (9)
Sporle CE Primary School, King's Lynn

Happiness

Happiness is yellow like a buttercup
It sounds like a rustling tree
It tastes like apple sauce
It smells like freshly baked bread
It looks like a pearl
It feels like silk
It reminds me of a wildflower meadow.

Samson Beech (9)
Sporle CE Primary School, King's Lynn

Sadness

Sadness is a dark, deep night
Sadness is death
Sadness is depressing and upsetting
Sadness is racism when people are called names
Sadness is bullying in the playground
Sadness is horrible.

Joseph Seale (11)
Turnditch CE Primary School, Turnditch

Sadness

Poverty, death, crying and hunger,
Young women weeping as their child slowly dies,
What is wrong with the world?
Surely we should be treated fairly.

Why should we fight wars with the rest of the world?
Can we not just be friends and get along?
Sadness and death lingers around every corner,
Millions die in wars,
Why, oh why can't people be friends?

But no, we can't just be friends,
The world can't get on,
Sadness is always there.

Molly Jones (10)
Turnditch CE Primary School, Turnditch

Netball

Bounce pass,
High pass,
Low pass,
Chest pass,
Obstruction!

Centre pass,
High class,
Got the ball,
Please don't fall,
Drop ball,
Never sure,
What ref will do!

Running up to get the ball,
Near the post, a minute left,
Three-all is the score,
All we need is one more
1 . . . 2 . . . 3
Score!

Amy Poynton & Chloe Ryan (10)
Turnditch CE Primary School, Turnditch

The Swallow

In the hedgerow where all is still,
Out pops a coloured bill,
Its silky body does take flight,
To hunt before the dead of night.
It flies and flies way up high,
To the peak of the murky sky,
Then the wind blows it everywhere,
Beating it without a care.
Its little heart beats faster and faster,
Then it stops from this disaster,
Suddenly it plummets to the ground,
Its heart stops with a pound.
It stays there like it is made of lead,
Poor little swallow, stone dead.

Daisy Warzynska (11)
Turnditch CE Primary School, Turnditch

Round The World

We start at England where we look down below,
We see all the people and say hello,
I look down below and there's a desert I know.
We fly over France and see Lyon's glance.
We land down in Spain for a drink of champagne.
We fly down to Cameroon to see a breed of baboon.
We go to Louisiana and see a cabana.
We travel to Melbourne and see koalas born.

Louis Curtis & George Wagstaff (9)
Turnditch CE Primary School, Turnditch

Birthdays Are . . .

Birthdays are . . .
Big balloons,
Massive party,
Go bowling,
Throw the ball, knock down 8 pins, 9 pins . . .
Strike!

Birthdays are . . .
Party poppers,
Huge cake,
Lots of pressies,
Pick a present, tear the paper, then . . .
A chocolate fountain!

Maria Webb (11)
Turnditch CE Primary School, Turnditch

Hallowe'en

H ave a fright
A ghost night
L iving dead
L ift up their head
O ut in the night
W erewolves give you a fright
E vil roams
E lves knock, looking for new homes
N ow it's all over until next year!

Jack Sutton (10)
Turnditch CE Primary School, Turnditch

Bounce, Bounce, Boing, Boing!

Bounce,
Bounce,
Boing,
Boing!
One point to the Blues,
Up the pitch, down the pitch,
Across the pitch, along the pitch,
The crowd are getting excited!

Bounce,
Bounce,
Boing,
Boing!
One point to the Reds,
The whistle blows half-time, five minutes
One-all,
The game gets going again,
The Blues defend well,
They've received the ball,
The Blues score,
The whistle blows, end of match.
The Blues win 2-1.

Emma White (10) & Lucy Phillips (11)
Turnditch CE Primary School, Turnditch

Sadness

Sadness is a foul, bitter-tasting mood,
Sadness is hunger in faraway countries,
Sadness is a cold, blue feeling,
Sadness sounds like a child sobbing,
Sadness is about poverty and racism,
Sadness is neglect and fear,
Sadness is a deep heart pounding,
Sadness is all around wherever you are!

Daniel Breeze (10)
Turnditch CE Primary School, Turnditch

Kennings

Winged lizard,
Flying assassin,
Fire breather,
Smoke sniffer,
Life predator,
Human reaper,
Meat eater,
Bone grinder,
Armoured dinosaur,
Claw bearer,
Man slaughterer,
Blood sprayer,
Air guardian,
Wind gladiator,
Earth splinterer,
Terror spreader,
Skeleton crusher,
Treasure guarder,
Creature of legend,
Animal of myths,
Symbol of China.

George Gibson
Wisborough Green Primary School, Wisborough Green

Kennings

Heart snatcher,
Claw smasher,
Breath stinker,
Cave seeker,
Night flier,
Clawed killer,
Moon eater,
Cruel savage.

Bethany Tidd (11)
Wisborough Green Primary School, Wisborough Green

Alone

I am bewildered in the freezing cold
I am heartbroken
I am cold and puzzled
I feel like I am dying with hunger
Sitting on a brick wall at night
I am terror-struck
I'm isolated
I need food
Glorious food
I'm anxious to try it
Confused
Unyielding
Deserted
Terror-struck
Mystified
I can see the people having a roast dinner
I am heartbroken and bewildered
I am cold and puzzled
I am destroyed and terror-struck
I'm shivering like an ice block in the winter
I am confused and isolated
I am poor
I am scared.

Alex Cooper
Wisborough Green Primary School, Wisborough Green

My Friendship Poem

F riends are always there for you
R eliable
I like friends because they help us
E veryone should have a friend
N ever be nasty to your friends
D o the right thing by them
S pecial friends are like gold dust.

Jack Dixon (7)
Wisborough Green Primary School, Wisborough Green

Neglected

Neglected
I looked up at the moon
My only friend

Neglected
I rolled over
On the cold, wet pathway

Neglected
I felt a tear drop
Drizzled down my cheek

Neglected
My bones stiffened
In the cold winter's night

Neglected
I saw a child
Place juicy turkey
Into his mouth

Neglected
My body froze and drifted
Into the world above.

Lucy Ansell
Wisborough Green Primary School, Wisborough Green

My Friendship Poem

F unny's their second name
R eally kind and nice
I adore them
E specially because they always have a smile on their faces
N ice things to say to you
D oing things together makes me happy
S omething always happens.

Emily Cornell (7)
Wisborough Green Primary School, Wisborough Green

My Unloved Life

Freezing
Scared and isolated
I look up at the shiny, shimmering stars staring
At me
Unhappy
Scared and isolated
Nobody to talk to
I watch as the boisterous boys
Stuff the fat, mouth-watering turkey into their dribbling mouths
Frightened
Scared and isolated
My stomach rumbles
It aches like mad
I fall onto the snow-covered, slippery, slimy road
My eyes fade and my legs tremble
Unloved
Scared and isolated
My heart sinks and a tear falls down my sore cheek
Worried
Scared and isolated
Scared, scared.

Hollie James (10)
Wisborough Green Primary School, Wisborough Green

My Friendship Poem

F riends are always together
R eally best friends stay together
I like being with my best friend
E very time I see my best friend, she always makes me laugh
N ever let your friend down
D on't be mean to your best friend
S omeone gets hurt, your best friend will always be there for you.

Grace Elsworth-Smith (7)
Wisborough Green Primary School, Wisborough Green

My Poor Life

Pain and discomfort
No passion or joy
Just a ragged T-shirt
But I'm only a boy.

Happiness and laughter
Not meant for me
Just rejection and pain
And no food for tea.

Drab and frosty
The pain too much to bear
I can't go on
And nobody to care.

As the moon goes out
Stars sparkle in the sky
Not a whisper or shout
But why?

Lise Easton (11)
Wisborough Green Primary School, Wisborough Green

My Friendship Poem

F riends look after you
R eally good friends
I like Natasha and Elena
E mily is nice
N atasha is my best friend
D o not upset your friends
S pecial friends are precious.

Lauren Porter (7)
Wisborough Green Primary School, Wisborough Green

Unwanted

Unwanted,
Desperate and scared,
I looked up to see twinkling stars
Turning and twisting in the dark blue sky,
The moon looked down at me,
He was my only friend.

Unwanted,
Sad and alone,
Why did this have to be me?
No friends, not even mice,
Freezing, all alone,
On slabs as cold as ice.

Unwanted,
Terrified and neglected,
Lying in the damp and cold.
Would anyone care?
Watching children eat juicy beef
Around a warm fire.

Unwanted,
Emotional and lonely,
I felt a salty tear roll down my face.
As my teeth chattered, I got colder,
Watching people
As they grew older.

Unwanted,
Glum and distraught,
I rolled onto my side,
As I saw a shooting star,
Maybe it was a sign of a brighter future.

Karis Montague (10)
Wisborough Green Primary School, Wisborough Green

The Forgotten Night

Lights gleamed in the windows
Shouts and laughter crawled down streets
I felt alone
I felt upset
I felt forgotten
The snow floated down
The frost bit cold
I felt frozen
I felt scared
I felt forgotten
Decorations were up
The ice frozen
I felt abandoned
I felt hungry
I felt forgotten
The roads were bare
The ghostly mist surrounded me
I felt broken
I felt unwanted
I felt forgotten
I peered through a window
A candle shone
A memory came back
I felt lonely
I felt tearful
I felt forgotten
I realise now my life is ruined
I realise now there's no going back
I realise now I'm forgotten forever.

Violet Nicholls (10)
Wisborough Green Primary School, Wisborough Green

Freezing At Christmas

I was rooted to the spot
I saw a child in a window dancing like an angel
Tears flowed steadily
I was stripped of all hope
I was forlorn
Terrified of what the future held
Snow started to fall
Dancing gently from the sky
I was under the Christmas tree
I remember when I was like that child dancing merrily in the window
Eating lots of food and receiving lots of toys
But those happy times are gone.

Clive Allen (11)
Wisborough Green Primary School, Wisborough Green

My Friendship Poem

F unny friends
R eally weird
I am happy when I see them
E xcellent friends
N ice friends
D on't make them cry
S pecial friends.

Zsuzsi Overton
Wisborough Green Primary School, Wisborough Green

Last Night

Isolated
Neglected
As I sat down on the tiles
That had a layer of ice.
I looked in a window
I saw a family
They had dignity.
Heartbroken
Crestfallen
My haggard body tried to sleep
But tears stopped my eyelids from closing.
The inside of me was sabotaged
Disconsolate
Lachrymose
I heaved my crestfallen body
To the bridge
Where I fell asleep
And never woke up.

Max Dillon
Wisborough Green Primary School, Wisborough Green

My Friendship Poem

F riends are really good to have
R eal friends are very funny
I love my friends
E ggs are fun to find with your friends
N atasha is really, really funny
D oing stuff with your friends is fun
S illy friends are really silly.

Isobel Mayhew (7)
Wisborough Green Primary School, Wisborough Green

A Victorian Child

Neglected and alone
Deserted
The cold pavement under my feet
The laugh of a child
The hiss of a train
The dirt on the pavement under my feet
The image of my family flashing in my mind
Gone forever and never to return
The loneliness, the bitterness
The terror of it all
How did it come to this?

Callum Pearson (10)
Wisborough Green Primary School, Wisborough Green

Alone

Agony
Isolated
How did I get in this chaos?
Kicked out
One false move and comfort left me behind
A cold tear
Ran down my face
As my family came in my mind
I closed my eyes
And drifted to sleep
I was all alone.

Richard Mason (10)
Wisborough Green Primary School, Wisborough Green

Neglected

N o one loves me
E veryone has love but me
G lumly I sit on my sack
L ovely smells of food fill my nose
E xcitement comes - and it goes
C aring for me was so long in the past
T he moon smiled down as my prayers echoed in the night
E veryone has love but me
D esperate and deserted, I look into a warm, welcoming window.

Alice Warwick (10)
Wisborough Green Primary School, Wisborough Green

I Am Alone

I am alone
In the sheer cold
Morbid
Watching the children in their warm houses
Jealous
No one with me
I am alone
Isolated
Pitch-black
No one to hold
Wrath
Lying on the pavement
Down
I am alone!

George Steere (10)
Wisborough Green Primary School, Wisborough Green

My Friendship Poem

F unny
R eally nice
I love my friends
E ven when I'm sad, my friend cheers me up
N obody should not have a friend
D on't hurt you
S wimming with them.

Joshua Rawlins (7)
Wisborough Green Primary School, Wisborough Green

My Friendship Poem

F riends are the best
R eally kind
I love Ethan
E than is the best
N atasha is my friend
D aniel is best
S am is the best football player ever.

Harry Baker (7)
Wisborough Green Primary School, Wisborough Green

My Friendship Poem

F riends are funny
R eally care for them
I love going to the park with my friends
E veryone can be friends
N obody can't be friends
D on't be nasty
S mile at them.

Jacob Ball (7)
Wisborough Green Primary School, Wisborough Green

My Friendship Poem

F riends always care for you
R oses are nice to give your friends when they are feeling ill
I zzy cares for me and never leaves me out
E aster is fun with your friends
N ovember is fun with your friends
D izzy friends are fun to play with
S wimming is fun with your friends.

Laura Travers
Wisborough Green Primary School, Wisborough Green

My Friendship Poem

F riends are very important
R eliable
I ncredibly fun friends
E njoyable company
N ever unkind
D o always play with you
S pecial friends will always be there for you.

James Cheal (8)
Wisborough Green Primary School, Wisborough Green

My Friendship Poem

F riends are funny all the time
R eally fun to play with
I need friends or I'd be lonely
E njoyable friends needed
N ever ever be mean to me
D o things in school with them
S o we always play together.

Natasha Calder Smith
Wisborough Green Primary School, Wisborough Green

My Friendship Poem

F riends are great to have
R eal friends are funny
I have loads of friends
E very friend is special
N ow play with your friends
D izzy friends
S wim with your friends.

Isobel Russel
Wisborough Green Primary School, Wisborough Green

My Friendship Poem

F riends are my best things to have
R eally, really kind
I love my friends very much
E specially when they play with me
N oisy friends are very good
D oing lots of things together
S ay sorry to other friends.

Hannah Kirby (7)
Wisborough Green Primary School, Wisborough Green

Being Alone

Being alone
Every day is a struggle
I want to be loved
All I want is to be loved
Love would be just glorious
One day I will have a family too
Eager to be loved.

Maddie Todd (9)
Wisborough Green Primary School, Wisborough Green

My Friendship Poem

F riends will play games with you, they will always be loyal.
R unning around the playground hurting yourself on the ground, friends will comfort you.
I n school, friends will help you if you get stuck.
E very day friends will be there for you and you will be there for them.
N othing is better than a friend. A games console wouldn't be loyal. A bottle of beer couldn't help if you were hurt.
D o not let your friends down, always be their friend.
S ome people are not friends and will let you down and blame you - they are not friends.

Harry Wheeler (9)
Wisborough Green Primary School, Wisborough Green

Kennings

Rainbow swirler,
Curvy curler,
Jewelled monster,
Savage sister,
Moon eater,
Body beater,
Skydiver,
Slippery saliva.

Lucy Travers (11)
Wisborough Green Primary School, Wisborough Green

Neglected

Heartbroken
Neglected
No one there for me
Unwanted
Tearful
Just a young, scraggy boy with no home or family
Scared
Isolated
All I want is to see my mum
Just a picture would fill my heart with love
Jealous
Lonely
I turned my head and I saw a girl
Gobbling down a juicy piece of meat
I felt jealousy strike through me
Freezing
Cold
My teeth were chattering, my lips were blue
I was so cold it was hard to move
I felt so unlucky.

Danielle Naughton (10)
Wisborough Green Primary School, Wisborough Green

Young Writers Information

We hope you have enjoyed reading this book - and that you will continue to enjoy it in the coming years.

If you like reading and writing poetry drop us a line, or give us a call, and we'll send you a free information pack.

Alternatively if you would like to order further copies of this book or any of our other titles, then please give us a call or log onto our website at www.youngwriters.co.uk

Young Writers Information
Remus House
Coltsfoot Drive
Peterborough
PE2 9JX
(01733) 890066